Cultural Atlas for Young People

FIRST CIVILIZATIONS

Erica C. D. Hunter, PH.D.

Facts On File®

AN INFOBASE HOLDINGS COMPANY

For Andromeda:
Editorial Director: Graham Bateman
Senior Art Editor: Steve McCurdy
Cartographic Manager: Olive Pearson
Cartographic Editor: Caroline Simpson
Cartographer: Richard Watts
Production Director: Clive Sparling
Typesetter: Brian Blackmore

For Lionheart Books:
Managing Editor: Lionel Bender
Art Editor: Ben White
Designer: Malcolm Smythe
Text Editor: Miles Litvinoff
Assistant Editor: Madeleine Samuel

AN ANDROMEDA BOOK

Planned and produced by:
Andromeda Oxford Limited
11–15 The Vineyard, Abingdon,
Oxfordshire OX14 3PX, England

Prepared by Lionheart Books

Library of Congress Cataloging-in-Publication
Data
Hunter, Erica C. D.
    First civilizations / Erica C. D. Hunter
      p.   cm, – (Cultural atlas for young
      people)
    Includes bibliographical references and
      index.
      1. Middle East–History–To 622–
    Juvenile literature. 2. Middle East–
    Antiquities–Juvenile literature. I. Title.
    II. Series.
    DS62.23.H86   1994
939'.4–dc20   93-41079

ISBN 0-8160-2976-8

Published in the United States by
Facts On File, Inc.
460 Park Avenue South
New York, N.Y. 10016

Facts On File books are available at special
discounts when purchased in bulk quantities for
businesses, associations, institutions or sales
promotions. Please call our Special Sales
Department in New York at 212/683-2244 (dial
800/322-8755 except in NY, AK or HI)

Origination by Eray Scan, Singapore

Printed in Belgium by Proost N.V. Turnhout

10 9 8 7 6 5 4 3 2 1

This book is printed on acid-free paper

Artwork and Picture Credits
Maps drafted by Alan Mais, Hornchurch, Essex.

Key: t = top, b = bottom, c = center, l = left, r = right etc.

1 M/Erich Lessing. 5 MH. 8 Photo RMN. 8–9 John Hillelson
Agency/Georg Gerster. 10 RHPL/Michael Jenner. 12 AA&A.
13 Institute of Archaeology, University of London. 19
Hutchison Library. 20 SH/F H C Birch. 21 SH. 22t MH. 22b
MH. 23t MH. 23b MH. 24t Picturepoint. 24bl David Stronach,
Berkely. 24br SH. 25 Andromeda. 26 Andromeda. 27tl
Andromeda. 27tr Hirmer Verlag. 28l Andromeda. 28r BM. 29
David & Joan Oates. 33 Z/K Goebel. 34 Scala. 36bl RHPL/V
Southwell. 36br Il Quadrante Edizione, Milan. 36tl
Ashmolean Museum. 38cl Photo RMN. 38cr Photo RMN.
38tc John Ridgeway. 38tr John Ridgeway. 40t Ashmolean
Museum. 40b Giraudon. 43t Claus Hansmann. 43cl
Andromeda. 43cr AA&A. 44tc BM. 44tr Scala. 44b AA&A. 45t
BM. 45b Scala. 48t Picturepoint. 48b Oriental Institute
Museum, Chicago. 49l Photo RMN. 49r Explorer/Fiore. 50–1

MH. 53t Scala. 53b Claus Hansmann. 55 Ashmolean
Museum. 56 Photo RMN. 57 MH. 59tl MH. 59r MH. 60 Photo
RMN. 61 Michael Roaf. 63 Ashmolean Museum. 64 MH. 65tl
Photo RMN. 65tr SH. 65cl David Harris. 67 SH/Jane Taylor.
68 Scala. 68–9 Ashmolean Museum. 69 Time
Magazine/Barry Iverson. 71t BM. 71b MH. 73 MH. 74
Michael Roaf. 75t Erica C D Hunter. 75b MH. 76t Photo
RMN. 76b MH. 77 Ashmolean Museum. 79tl Z/C Skrein/M
Epp. 79r BM. 81tl M/Erich Lessing. 81tr Erica C D Hunter.
83t RHPL. 83b RHPL. 85 M/Erich Lessing. 86t MH. 86b
M/Erich Lessing. 87 Photo RMN. 88 Michael Roaf. 89 Z. 90t
BM. 90b BM. 91t BM. 91b BM

List of abbreviations
AA&A Ancient Art & Architecture Collection, Middlesex, UK.
BM British Museum, London, UK. M Magnum Photos
Limited, London, UK. MH Michael Holford, Essex, UK. RHPL
Robert Harding Picture Library, London, UK. SH Sonia
Halliday Photographs, Buckinghamshire, UK. Z Zefa Picture
Library, London, UK

CONTENTS

INTRODUCTION

This book is about Mesopotamia – the land between the Tigris and Euphrates rivers – and the ancient Near East. It covers the present-day country of Iraq, as well as parts of Iran, Turkey, Syria, Lebanon and Israel. The region is varied in geography and climate, ranging from deserts to forested mountains and fertile river plains.

More than 12,000 years ago people of this region were among the first to change from a hunting-and-gathering, wandering lifestyle to settled farming communities. Many of the plants and animals on which modern European agriculture is based were first domesticated (brought under human control) in the Near East.

The first cities in the world also emerged in Mesopotamia, by about 4000 BC, and influenced the surrounding cultures. The ancient Greeks and Romans learned from Mesopotamian civilization, and passed on their cultural heritage to Europe. For this reason Mesopotamia has been called the "cradle of civilization."

In recent times the Near East, unique in its contribution to human history, has been the scene of conflict: first the Iran–Iraq War, and then the Gulf War of 1991. Many wars have been fought in Mesopotamia from earliest times. The first kings, dating from about 3000 BC, were originally leaders chosen by the people to defend city-states in times of war. By 2300 BC kings had become permanent heads of state, attending not only to military matters but also to the welfare of the population.

Rulers were thought to be responsible to the gods, even though some of them, such as the Assyrian, Babylonian and Persian kings, ruled vast empires. The empire of Darius III was conquered by Alexander the Great in 331 BC. From then on, the civilization of the ancient Near East went into decline, to be replaced by the newly powerful Hellenistic (Greek-speaking) culture.

Abbreviations used in this book
BC = Before Christ. c. = circa (about). mi = miles.
ft = feet. in = inches.

First Civilizations is divided into two parts. Part One, **The Land and the People**, traces the development of hunter-gatherer societies through village life to urban (city) life. It describes the domestication of plants and animals, and technological inventions such as clay bricks and pottery and the first writing. Part Two, **Kingdoms and Empires**, charts the rise and fall of the great kingdoms and empires of the Near East. These began with the reign of the Semitic king Sargon of Agade (2334–2279 BC) and ended with the Persian dynasty.

Most of the evidence for the history of Mesopotamia and the surrounding cultures comes from archaeological excavations. Special features in the book focus on the contribution of outstanding sites.

Maps are an important part of the book. In Part One they show where technological changes began and spread in the Near East. In Part Two they show how empires grew and then faded, to be replaced by others. Location maps accompany each special spread, so that the sites may be easily identified.

Many of the pages list the names and dates of the cultures and kings of the period. Kings are usually grouped according to the dynasty (ruling family or line) to which they belonged. The spelling of names is often uncertain, and other versions can be found. Sargon, for example, may also be written as Sharruken. In *First Civilizations* the easiest and most popular form of these names has usually been used. Similarly, many of the dates are not definite and should only be used as an approximate guide.

The Glossary on page 92 explains archaeological and technical terms and also defines the names of periods and dynasties. The Gazetteer on page 93 lists sites in alphabetical order, giving their latitude and longitude, as well as their modern locations.

The section entitled Further Reading provides a list of books that we hope will interest you after reading *First Civilizations*.

▷ Cuneiform script carved over the relief sculpture from a 9th-century BC site at Kalhu.

TABLE OF DATES

	12,000 BC	10,000 BC	7000 BC	4000 BC	3000 BC
Events in MESOPOTAMIA * denotes important site of the period ▲ denotes a king words <u>underlined</u> are historical periods	End of Ice Age *Shanidar Cave	*Zawi Chemi Shanidar	<u>Hassuna, Samarra, Halaf, Ubaid</u>	<u>Uruk</u> *Tell Madhhur *Ur	<u>Jamdat Nasr</u> *Mari <u>Early Dynastic</u> Nippur *Uruk

ARCHEOLOGICAL PERIOD	EPI-PALEOLITHIC (MESOLITHIC)	PROTO-NEOLITHIC	ACERAMIC NEOLITHIC	NEOLITHIC	EARLY BRONZE AGE SUMERIAN

TECHNICAL INVENTIONS

Hunting and gathering	Villages	Ox-plow	Cities	City-states
Dog domesticated	Basketry	Cattle domesticated	Donkeys domesticated	Lost-wax method of casting metal
Microlithic flint tools	Grain roasting	Potter's wheel	Carts	Gold- and silversmithi
	Sheep herded	Baked mud-bricks	Copper weapons	
	Farming – grain crops	Pottery kilns	Cylinder seals	
	Mud-bricks	Irrigation	Cuneiform writing	
	Weaving	Boats		
	Pottery			
	Early copper tools			

Stone bird head from Nemrik c.7500 BC

Flint arrowheads from Tell Brak

Susa A bowl c.4000 BC

Metal daggers from the Royal Cemetery of Ur c.2600 BC

ART AND ARCHITECTURE

Round huts	Stone sculptures		Cone mosaics
	Rectangular houses	Tripartite temples	"Uruk Mona Lisa"
Plastered skulls			"Warka vase"
	Clay figurines	Walled cities	Palaces

Events in the LEVANT	*Mt Carmel	*Jericho	<u>Halaf</u> <u>Ubaid</u>		

Events in IRAN				*Choga Mami	

Bronze and silver stag fro Alaca Huyuk, c.2300 BC

Events in ANATOLIA				*Chatai Huyuk	

Events in EGYPT					Pre-Dynastic

Printed stone mask from Nahal Hemar c.10,000 BC

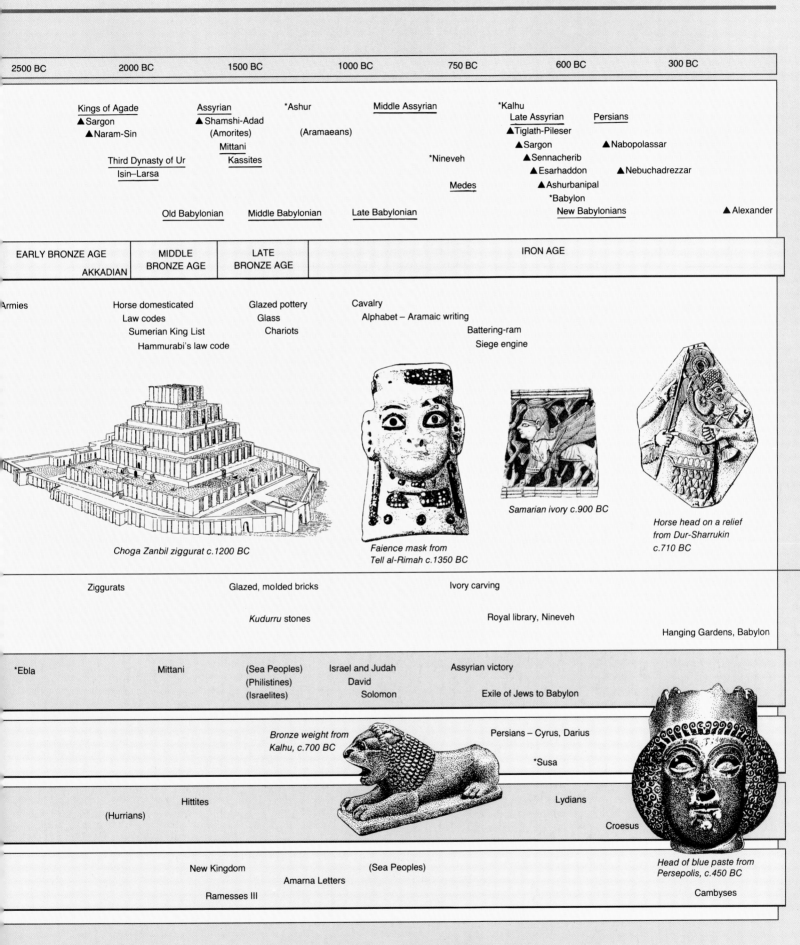

2500 BC	2000 BC	1500 BC	1000 BC	750 BC	600 BC	300 BC

Kings of Agade · ▲Sargon · ▲Naram-Sin

Assyrian · ▲Shamshi-Adad (Amorites) · Mittani · Kassites

*Ashur · (Aramaeans)

Middle Assyrian

*Nineveh · Medes

*Kalhu · Late Assyrian · ▲Tiglath-Pileser · ▲Sargon · ▲Sennacherib · ▲Esarhaddon · ▲Ashurbanipal · *Babylon · New Babylonians

Persians · ▲Nabopolassar · ▲Nebuchadrezzar

▲Alexander

Third Dynasty of Ur · Isin–Larsa

Old Babylonian · Middle Babylonian · Late Babylonian

EARLY BRONZE AGE / AKKADIAN	MIDDLE BRONZE AGE	LATE BRONZE AGE	IRON AGE

Armies

Horse domesticated · Law codes · Sumerian King List · Hammurabi's law code

Glazed pottery · Glass · Chariots

Cavalry · Alphabet – Aramaic writing · Battering-ram · Siege engine

Choga Zanbil ziggurat c.1200 BC

Faience mask from Tell al-Rimah c.1350 BC

Samarian ivory c.900 BC

Horse head on a relief from Dur-Sharrukin c.710 BC

Ziggurats

Glazed, molded bricks

Kudurru stones

Ivory carving

Royal library, Nineveh

Hanging Gardens, Babylon

*Ebla

Mittani

(Sea Peoples) · (Philistines) · (Israelites)

Israel and Judah · David · Solomon

Assyrian victory · Exile of Jews to Babylon

Bronze weight from Kalhu, c.700 BC

Persians – Cyrus, Darius

*Susa

(Hurrians)

Hittites

Lydians · Croesus

New Kingdom · Amarna Letters · Ramesses III

(Sea Peoples)

Head of blue paste from Persepolis, c.450 BC · Cambyses

PART ONE

THE LAND AND THE PEOPLE

△ An Akkadian relief from about 2300 BC showing naked prisoners of war.

▷ Stairs leading to the top of the ziggurat at Ur, where once a temple stood.

PHYSICAL BACKGROUND

The lands where the first civilizations developed stretched from The Gulf (often known as the Persian Gulf) through modern Iraq, to Syria and the Levant (present-day Lebanon and Israel) on the Mediterranean coast. This area of the Near East is often called the Fertile Crescent.

The heartland of this cradle of human history was Mesopotamia – the flat plain of rich soil that was watered by the Tigris and Euphrates rivers. These two rivers rise in the mountainous region of northeastern Turkey and drain into The Gulf.

The Zagros Mountains in modern Iran formed the eastern barrier to this region. In the west and south were the desolate lands of the Syrian and Arabian deserts.

Climate and environment
When the last Ice Age ended, in about 12,000 BC, the climate of the Near East became similar to what it is today. The vegetation (plant life) changed because of the warmer temperatures.

The mountains of Iran, Turkey, and the Mediterranean coast became forested with oak, cedar, and pine trees. These woods and forests became the home of deer, wild sheep and goats, wolves, and leopards. Wild wheat and barley also grew here.

The northern part of Mesopotamia consisted of rolling grasslands where boars, oxen, and even lions roamed. The southern part of Mesopotamia, towards The Gulf, hosted a wealth of bird life that lived in its many swamps and marshes.

Water
People could only live permanently in the areas where there were constant supplies of water. Rainfall was scarce in Mesopotamia, but the Tigris and Euphrates were mighty rivers, fed by the melting snows of the Zagros and Taurus mountains. With their many lesser, tributary rivers, they provided a lifeline throughout Mesopotamia.

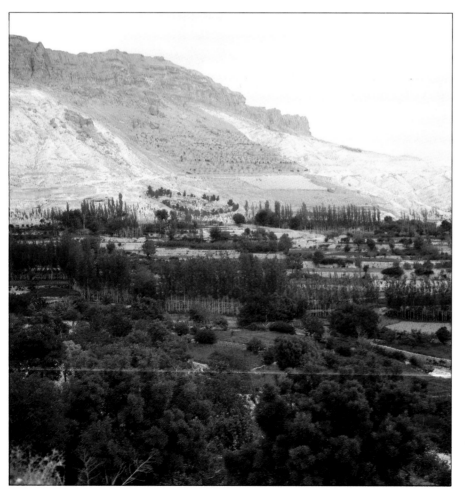

◁ An oasis in Syria. Oases – areas that are fertile because water is present – are quite common in deserts. Often the water comes from an underground spring. Palm trees occur naturally at oases, and with irrigation crops can be grown, allowing orchards and gardens to thrive.

Scale 1: 14 280 000

Irrigation
Unlike the river Nile, which flooded Egypt with such regularity that it could be calculated, the Tigris and Euphrates were unpredictable and unreliable. They could rise in flood, becoming raging muddy torrents, or change their courses overnight and in doing so destroy the villages that lined their banks.

In time, the people of the river plains learned to build irrigation systems (canals and ditches) that helped them control the flow of water and channel it to their food crops. Then the "land between the rivers" (which is what the Greek name Mesopotamia means) became highly productive for farming.

C
D
E
F
G
H

Black Sea

CAUCASUS MTS

Caspian Sea

Kara Kum

Amu Darya

il Irmak

SYRIA

Habur

Great Zab

Tigris

ELBURZ MTS

Euphrates

MESOPOTAMIA

ZAGROS MOUNTAINS

Dasht-e Kavir

SYRIAN DESERT

ELAM

Dasht-e Lut

An Nafud

The Gulf

ARABIA

HEJAZ

Gulf of Oman

ed
ea

Natural vegetation

- Coniferous forest
- Deciduous forest
- Mixed forest
- Mediterranean forest
- Floodplain
- Steppe
- Semi-desert
- Desert

△ Land and vegetation of the Near East. This map shows the natural vegetation, that is, how the vegetation would be if left alone, without human interference. The vegetation depends mainly on the pattern of rainfall. Large areas of the Near East receive so little rain that the land is desert and not suitable for human settlement. Fringes of the desert are steppe grasslands.

A
B
C
D

3

Black Sea

Caspian Sea

2

Euphrates

Tigris

Mediterranean Sea

1

Red Sea

The Gulf

Mean annual rainfall

inches
40
24
16
8
4
0

Scale 1 : 31 500 000

0   800km

0   500 miles

◁ Annual rainfall in the Near East. The region is mainly dry and hot. It receives no rain during the summer months from June to September. Temperatures are high and in the lower-lying zones often reach 113°F. In winter, snow falls on the mountains of the Levant, Turkey, and Iran.

11

ARCHAEOLOGY IN THE NEAR EAST

section from living tree

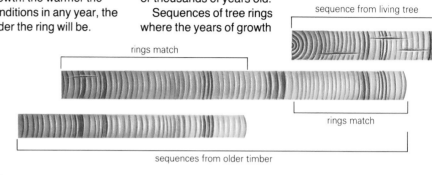

▽ The trunk of a tree shows a number of rings when it is sawn in half. Each ring equals a year's growth: the warmer the conditions in any year, the wider the ring will be.

By adding up the number of rings, the age of the tree can be worked out, even if it is hundreds or thousands of years old. Sequences of tree rings where the years of growth are known can be matched with the ring patterns of an ancient piece of timber, telling us how old it is.

sequence from living tree

rings match

rings match

sequences from older timber

time back in past

Archaeology is the scientific study of the human past using the physical traces left by early people. This has told us a lot about the history of the Near East. In the 19th century, archaeologists from Europe and America dug up sites to find objects for their museums. Today, archaeology tries to reconstruct from its findings how society was organized.

Excavating a site

Archaeologists do a variety of jobs, from supervising the people who physically dig the site to recording every detail about the different levels that are exposed. The oldest remains are usually at the lowest levels, with the most recent closest to the surface.

Archaeological "finds" may range from gold coins and beautiful jewelry to hundreds or thousands of pieces of broken pottery, fragments of animal bones, and tools made of stone (flint). Even the seeds of plants are collected, by passing the soil in which they are found through sieves. Seeds give information about crops and foods. Important finds that are broken are repaired, and there are special treatments for ivory, wood, metal items, and inscriptions (carved or engraved words).

The contours (outline) of excavated sites used to be mapped by hand, but nowadays they are often charted using a computer. More and more advanced scientific techniques are being used in archaeology today.

▷ A worker uses a paintbrush to dust away the soil from pieces of pottery. The woman is placing these pieces, called sherds, into the rubber basket. The pottery is taken away and washed carefully so that any decoration or inscriptions will not be removed. The location of each sherd is noted to help work out their relationship.

Many different tools are used to excavate a site. These range from large picks, hoes and spades, which are used for surface digging, to scalpels, dental picks, and tweezers for fine and intricate work. Rubber buckets are used to carry away the unwanted soil.

sieve

scalpel

tweezers

dental pick

small pick

hand broom

paint brushes

large pick

trowel

level

hoe

spade

surveyor's pole

tape measure

rubber bucket

◁ Archaeologists at work. The team have unearthed the stone wall topped by the layers of mud-brick. After they have drawn it, they will demolish it to find out what is underneath. A worker climbs the ladder with a bucket of soil, which is dumped on to the nearby piles. The dagger, skeleton, broken pots, and other items will be uncovered as the lower levels are excavated.

▽ Fragile objects that are found have to be very carefully treated. These statuettes were made from mud plastered on a reed framework. The intricate process of sticking together all the fragments is a painstaking and expensive job that takes months.

Building up a picture from the site

The layout of the buildings in the different layers of the excavation show archaeologists how the site developed. Major features, such as city walls and gates, may show similarities with other sites and help to establish the site's dating sequence or chronology.

The chronology also can be worked out from the pottery that was found, because certain shapes were used in different periods. Coins are very useful for working out the date of a site, but coins are not found in periods earlier than the 7th century BC. Inscriptions may also supply historical information.

Radio carbon dating, a sophisticated scientific technique, can show the age of wooden objects. However, the results may not be of great value for dating a site, because the objects may originally have come from elsewhere. They may therefore show trade links between the excavated site and other areas of the Near East. Imported pottery excavated from the site may supply similar evidence.

EARLY PEOPLES (to 11,000 BC)

In the Paleolithic or Old Stone Age, *Homo sapiens* or modern humans lived alongside Neanderthal humans (*Homo neanderthalensis*). Both groups lived as hunter-gatherers, obtaining their food by hunting wild animals and collecting plants and other edibles. They took shelter in caves, such as Mount Carmel (now in Israel) and Shanidar (now in Iraq).

After the last great Ice Age ended, *Homo sapiens* began to grow crops and to herd animals in the Near East in about 11,000–9000 BC. This change in food production happened over thousands of years, and people began to settle in permanent villages.

Near East Paleolithic and Mesolithic cultures
Cultures are represented by named archaeological sites and by layers in the ground where the appropriate objects were found.
Lower Paleolithic
85,000–60,000 BC   ACHEULEAN culture
Site: Shanidar Cave (Base), Iraq
Middle Paleolithic
60,000–35,000 BC   MOUSTERIAN culture
Site: Shanidar Cave (Layers D, C), Iraq
40,000 BC   *Homo sapiens* appears
Upper Paleolithic
35,000–18,000 BC   BARADOSTIAN cultures
Sites: Kebara (Layer D), Israel; Zarzi, Iraq
Epi-Paleolithic (Mesolithic)
18,000–12,000 BC   ZARZIAN culture
End of the last Ice Age
Sites: Kebara (Layers C, B), Israel; M'Lefaat, Iraq; Karim Shahir, Iraq; Shanidar Cave (Layer B), Iraq; Zawi Chemi Shanidar (B), Iraq; Mt Carmel, Israel.

▽ Early agriculture. Barley and wheat were first cultivated in the foothills of northern Mesopotamia between about 11,000 BC and 9000 BC. By 5000 BC, these crops were grown in the Caucasus to the north, in Egypt to the south, to the west in Anatolia (Turkey) and south-eastern Europe, and eastwards in Iran and even India. In China and south-east Asia, rice and millet were being cultivated.

Introduction of agriculture
- Before 9000 BC
- 9000–7000 BC
- 7000–5000 BC
- 5000–3000 BC

Principal crop
- Barley and wheat
- Millet
- Rice

Scale 1 : 20 740 000
0 — 600 km
0 — 400 miles

Equatorial scale
1 : 88 000 000

Area covered on main map

> The changing shape of The Gulf. The Gulf has been growing in size since 15,000 BC, when sea levels were about 330ft lower than today. As the last Ice Age ended, sea levels rose with the warmer temperatures. Since 4000 BC sea levels have remained almost the same, but silting from the Tigris and Euphrates rivers has changed the coastline. These maps show the boundaries of present-day countries.

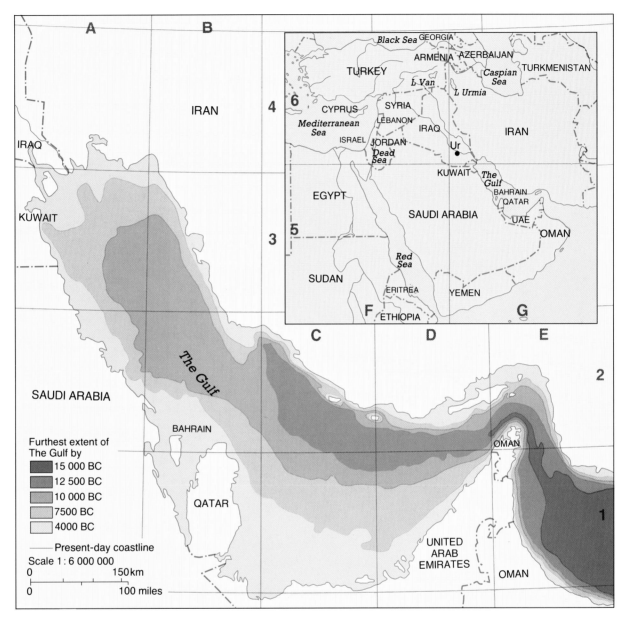

SAUDI ARABIA

BAHRAIN

QATAR

Furthest extent of The Gulf by
- 15 000 BC
- 12 500 BC
- 10 000 BC
- 7500 BC
- 4000 BC

— Present-day coastline
Scale 1 : 6 000 000

0 ———— 150km
0 ———— 100 miles

△ A snake painted on a piece of pottery dating from before 5000 BC. Many such pottery decorations show the wild animals and birds that lived in the ancient Near East.

The Neolithic revolution

The change from hunter-gatherer societies transformed the human lifestyle and is known as the "Neolithic revolution" (Neolithic means New Stone Age). The first settlements were in Palestine and the upper Euphrates valley of Syria. They seem to have developed separately rather than coming from a single center.

Climatic changes that took place in the Near East after the last Ice Age resulted in higher temperatures, different forms of vegetation and, perhaps, fewer animals. In the warmer temperatures the human population increased. The combination of these events may have helped trigger the Neolithic revolution.

Stone technology

To cater for the new methods of food production new tools had to be developed. Most tools were made from flint or other stone using such techniques as chipping, flaking, "pecking," and grinding.

Towards the end of the Paleolithic period, very small flints appeared. Called microliths, these come in different shapes. Some set in bone sickle handles (curved cutting tools) have been found at Mount Carmel. Microlith flints were sharper and more efficient than the larger tools of the Paleolithic or Old Stone Age. They show that people collected grains, but do not prove that they already cultivated plants.

15

MESOPOTAMIAN SITES

Shanidar

Shanidar Cave is located near the Great Zab river in the rugged Zagros Mountains of Iraqi Kurdistan. As early as 100,000 BC small groups of Neanderthal people sheltered here during the cold winter months. They hunted wild sheep, pigs, cattle, and goats.

Several of the cave-dwellers were killed by rockfalls. Pollen deposits found with skeletons show that Neanderthal people may have also buried their dead, sometimes with flowers. Their stone tools belong to the Middle Paleolithic Mousterian culture.

Modern humans (*Homo sapiens*) appeared at Shanidar in about 40,000 BC. Their tools were much more advanced than those of the Neanderthals, who died out by 33,000 BC. There are no signs of people living at Shanidar between 28,000 BC and 12,000 BC. Later tools from the Epi-Paleolithic culture found there are made of obsidian (a dark, glassy, volcanic rock), indicating trade with south-east Turkey. Twenty-six skeletons, some with grave goods, were buried in the cave in about 10,000 BC.

▽ Life at Zawi Chemi Shanidar. Hunters are gathered around the fire. One is making a flint spearhead, by flaking it into a sharp point. Another man has been collecting firewood from the nearby oak forests. The men wear garments made from animal skins. Skins were also used for the roofs of the round huts.

Zawi Chemi Shanidar

Zawi Chemi Shanidar, 1.8mi from Shanidar Cave, bridges the period between the Epi-Paleolithic and the first fully developed villages, such as Jarmo. The stone tools used were similar to earlier ones, but new types also emerged. As at Shanidar Cave, there was some trading in types of stone used for toolmaking.

At three different periods, round huts of about 13ft in diameter were built of river boulders. People may have lived at Zawi

▽ Women at Zawi Chemi Shanidar scrape and stretch the skin of a red deer. They may have also made the fiber baskets, used for collecting such food as snails, outside the hut doorways. Goats or sheep are kept behind the wicker fence.

Chemi Shanidar through the summer and returned to Shanidar Cave for the winter. Wild wheat and barley grew nearby, but crops may have been sown. Sheep were herded after about 10,000 BC probably being used for food.

A pile of eagles' wingbones and 15 goats' skulls were found at the site. This suggests that people practiced religious ceremonies there. Zawi Chemi Shanidar was settled at the same time as many sites in the Levant but there are no direct links.

EARLY VILLAGE LIFE

By 10,000 BC people began to settle in villages. Many of these villages were very small, covering less than 2.5 acres (about the area of a small field). Round huts were built sunk partly into the ground for insulation against extremes of heat and cold. The earliest group of round huts dates from as long ago as 15,000 BC at Ain Gev, on the banks of the Sea of Galilee. Much later, houses became rectangular with plastered walls, and they sometimes had several rooms. Both stages of housing were found among the 26 levels of occupation at Beidha in present-day southern Jordan.

Tools, materials, and crafts
People still made many tools from stone. Some had chisel edges and may have been used to cut wood, which was then fashioned into other tools. Wooden implements may have been used in harvesting or for animal traps. Unlike stone, wood decays, but at Nahal Hemar in modern Israel a wooden-handled sickle has been found.

Bone and horn from slaughtered animals made a variety of tools that were used for fishing, the preparation of hides (animal skins) and basketry, weaving, and rope-making.

Evidence of matting dating from as early as 10,000 BC has been found at Shanidar Cave.

Tools used by North American Indian tribes today show how these crafts were practiced.

Nahal Hemar
Some very useful finds have been made at Nahal Hemar, a cave in the Judaean desert near the Dead Sea. Until this discovery was made in 1938, the only evidence of reed matting and basketry was a few impressions left in clay.

Fragments of textiles, wood, and basketry dating from about 7000 BC were found in the cave. They had been preserved by the dry climate. Hundreds of pieces of cord, ranging from fine string to thick rope, show the high technical skills of the people at this site. Baskets made from coils of twisted cord and coated in bitumen (a naturally occurring tar) may have been used to carry and store water.

Among the ritual or religious objects unearthed at Nahal Hemar were a stone mask with a human head, heads made of wood and clay, four small carved bone human heads, and several adult skulls. These items may have been part of a cult of ancestor-worship, which was common among early peoples.

▽ This round house at Qermez Dere in northern Iraq was built partly sunk into the ground. Sunken houses were easier to build and also had better insulation against the climate. The roof, possibly made of skins, may have been held up by wooden poles. The stone walls were covered with mud. Cooking was done on the hearth. The stone-and-plaster pillar and the skulls indicate that ritual cults had developed.

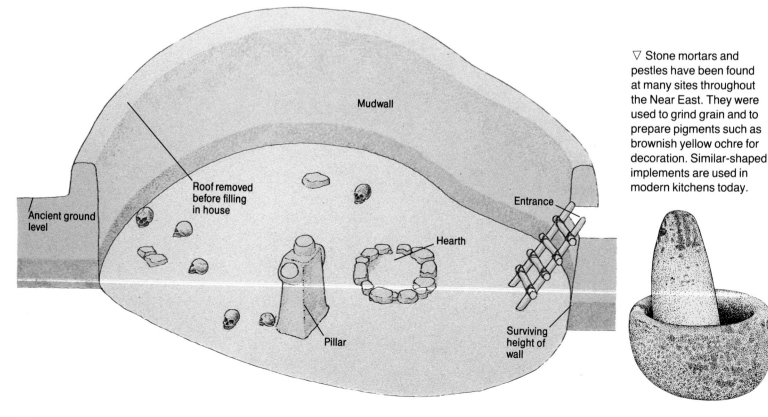

Mudwall

Roof removed before filling in house

Ancient ground level

Hearth

Entrance

Pillar

Surviving height of wall

▽ Stone mortars and pestles have been found at many sites throughout the Near East. They were used to grind grain and to prepare pigments such as brownish yellow ochre for decoration. Similar-shaped implements are used in modern kitchens today.

◁ Modern houses in villages in the Near East are still built of mud-brick. Their flat roofs, made of matting laid upon timber beams, can be used for living space, sleeping, and storage.

◁ Male and female statuettes from a large collection found at Ain Ghazal, near Amman in Jordan. They are made of reed plastered with clay. The exact purpose of these figures is unknown, but must have been linked to rituals or religious practice.

Widespread ritual cults

Plastered and decorated skulls, sometimes with shells in their eye sockets, have been found at many sites from the same period in the Levant, including Jericho, Ain Mallaha, Mount Carmel, and Ain Ghazal. At Nemrik, in northern Mesopotamia, 15 stylized stone sculptures of birds, animals, and humans were discovered. These may have been totems (symbolic objects used in rituals).

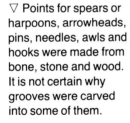

▽ Points for spears or harpoons, arrowheads, pins, needles, awls and hooks were made from bone, stone and wood. It is not certain why grooves were carved into some of them.

▷ Textiles were woven from plant fibers, probably flax (linen), in several ways. Pairs of weft threads were twisted around the warps to produce a dense weave called close twining (*top*). With spaced twining, the twisted threads were separated (*centre*). Normal or tabby weaving (*below*) was also carried out. Weaving was done by hand, using tools made from the long bones of animals. Shuttles that were pointed at one end and pierced with a hole at the other have been found at Ghassul in Jordan.

▽ Sickles were used to cut grasses and reeds. They were often made from bone. The tiny microlith flint blades were fixed to the handle with bitumen.

FIRST FARMERS (11,000–9300 BC)

The Near East was one of the first regions in the world where agriculture developed. Wild ancestors of the grains that were cultivated and the animals that were domesticated first appeared in the Levant and on the hills flanking the north Mesopotamian and Syrian plains.

Grain collection

The Neolithic revolution in the Levant began about 11,000 BC with the Natufian period. Sickles and grinding stones from this period found at Mount Carmel, on the shores of the Mediterranean, indicate that cereals were an important part of the diet. At Ain Mallaha, in Syria, a number of bell-shaped storage pits were discovered. These were lined with plaster and used to store grain. At Mureybet in northern Syria there were pits to roast grain. It is not known whether these cereals were cultivated or only gathered.

◁ The first farmers probably winnowed their grain (to separate edible grain from outer chaff) as this present-day Arab farmer. His fork may be based on an ancient design. Few early wooden tools have been found.

▽ Settlements and farmers. After the last Ice Age, people began to establish villages in areas of good rainfall (more than 8 in a year) where cereals grew naturally and animals were plentiful. Such early village sites span the Fertile Crescent from the Levant through northern Syria to Iraqi Kurdistan.

Legend:
- Epi-Paleolithic site, 18 000–9300 BC
- Proto-Neolithic site, 9300–8500 BC
- Aceramic Neolithic site, 8500–7000 BC
- Distribution of wild barley and wheat
- Distribution of sheep and goats
- Annual rainfall over 8 inches

Scale 1: 9 000 000

0   300 km

0   200 miles

▷ The Taurus Mountains
dominate this valley in
Cilicia, southern Turkey.
It lies in the rainfall zone
where crops could be
grown in the fields without
irrigation. Herds could
graze in the pastures
during the winter months
and in the summer were
taken up the mountains to
feed. The environment
provides a year-round food
supply.

▽ Stages in the
domestication of wheat in
the Near East. Emmer
wheat was a natural hybrid
(cross-bred offspring) of
einkorn wheat and goat
grass. Further selective
breeding helped produce
wheat plants ideal for
harvesting and threshing.

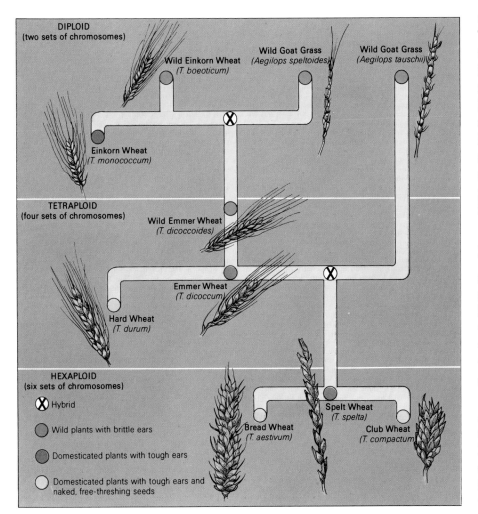

Grain cultivation

The Natufian diet included wild barley and
two kinds of wheat that grew naturally in the
Near East. Einkorn wheat and emmer wheat
must have provided the seed for the first crops.
Domestic varieties of wheat were developed
over generations of selective planting and
harvesting. Other cereals, such as barley, were
also bred to create strains that yielded more
seed. This selection process helped people to
produce more food. By 8000 BC most communities in the Near East grew cereals.

Animal husbandry

We cannot tell exactly when people first bred
animals – the process of domestication took
several thousand years and was complicated.
Many animals that were native to the Near East
were eventually domesticated: for example,
wolves were domesticated to become dogs,
"mouflons" became sheep, and aurochs (wild
cattle) became cows.

Natufian sites including Mount Carmel and
Abu Hureyra in Syria show that wild animals
(gazelle, boar, deer) were commonly eaten.
Large quantities of bones from young animals
could suggest that herding and selective cull-
ing (choosing which animals would remain in
the herd) were taking place.

ANIMALS IN DAILY LIFE

Dogs seem to have been the first animals that were tamed. A dog's jawbone from 11,000 BC has been found at Palegawra in northeastern Iraq. At Ain Mallaha a skeleton of a young puppy dated to 10,000 BC was buried in a grave with a woman. Dogs were domesticated from wolves and probably helped people hunt wild animals.

Sheep and goats

Not all wild animals could be domesticated. Large amounts of bones left at Natufian sites in the Levant show that gazelles were a major part of the diet. Attempts to herd them seem to have failed, and instead sheep, which were not native to the region, were introduced from northern zones.

Sheep and goats formed an important part of the farming economy, providing meat, hides, milk, and fleece. The first domestic sheep appear in about 11,000 BC at Zawi Chemi Shanidar. Goats were domesticated at Tepe Asiab, in the Zagros Mountains.

These animals also had a ritual or religious importance. Goats' skulls were found at Zawi Chemi Shanidar, along with wing bones of large birds. Two rams' skulls were found attached, one above the other, to the walls of a shrine at Ganj Dareh.

△ A procession of goats, sheep, and cattle, inlaid in bone on the "Standard of Ur" (probably the sounding box of a musical instrument). The men's clothes shown here were made from the fine wool of domesticated sheep, which was much softer than the rough hairy fleece of wild sheep.

▽ Arab warriors on camels fleeing from the Assyrian army. Camels were introduced into Mesopotamia from Arabia between 2000 BC and 1000 BC. They were used for transport and war.

Origin of common farm animals			
Domesticated animal	Wild ancestor	Region	Date
Dog	Wolf	Near East	c. 11,000 BC
Goat	Bezoar goat	Near East	c. 8500 BC
Sheep	Asiatic mouflon	Near East	c. 8000 BC
Pig	Wild boar	Near East	c. 7500 BC
Cattle	Auroch	Near East	c. 7000 BC
Cat	Wild cat	Near East	c. 7000 BC
Chicken	Red jungle fowl	China	c. 6000 BC
Llama	Guanaco	Andes	c. 5000 BC
Donkey	Wild ass	Near East	c. 4000 BC
Horse	Tarpan	Southern Russia	c. 4000 BC
Camel	Wild camel	?Southern Arabia/ ?Southern Central Asia	c. 3000 BC
Guinea-pig	Cavy	Peru	c. 2000 BC
Rabbit	Wild rabbit	Spain	c. 1000 BC
Turkey	Wild turkey	Mexico	c. 300 BC

Cattle

Wild cattle (aurochs) roamed the Near East and were hunted for their meat and hides. At Chatal Hüyuk in central Turkey, cattle were domesticated by 6000 BC. They were an important source of food and make up 90 percent of the animal bones found at this site.

Bulls' skulls have been found in several shrines. In one, they were near a painting of vultures attacking headless corpses. At Mureybit in northern Syria, fragments of an ox's skull were deliberately buried in a clay bench. In Anatolia the bull became associated with the weather or storm god.

▷ A fine relief of a mastiff being taken out hunting. Hunting dogs were bred for size and strength. Dog skeletons found in graves at Eridu, Iraq, and dating from about 5000 BC have been identified as greyhounds. They are the ancestors of the saluki, which is still prized today in Arabia for its hunting skills.

◁ A 9th-century BC carving showing horses being groomed and fed. The onager or wild ass was native to the Near East. But the horse only arrived from the central Russian steppes in about 4000 BC. Horses were used at first to pull chariots. In Sumerian times (about 2500 BC) they were thought to be inferior beasts which no gentleman would ride. A king or a noble would ride in a chariot pulled by asses. By 1000 BC, however, cavalry formed very effective fighting units.

BUILDERS, POTTERS, AND TRADE

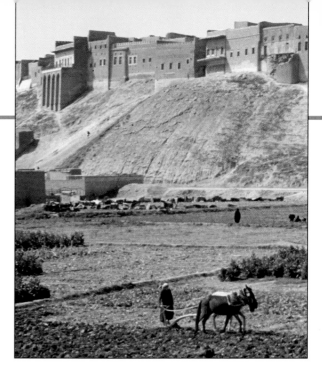

People first used unbaked mud-brick for building in about 8000 BC. It was cheap, easy to make, and more readily available than stone. The earliest bricks, from the Proto-Neolithic period (the earliest Neolithic), were made by hand and looked like a loaf of bread, with a flat base and a rounded top. Much later, houses became rectangular in shape when straight-sided mud-bricks were used.

Jericho

People lived at Jericho, in the Jordan valley, from 9000 BC. Round huts built from cigar-shaped handmade bricks provide the earliest known use of mud-bricks. In about 8000 BC a huge, thick, stone wall was erected, surrounded by a large ditch. There was also a massive tower with a staircase inside. The wall and tower were probably built for defense and were recalled in the later biblical story of Joshua.

▷ The city of Erbil in Iraqi Kurdistan stands on a mound over 165ft high. Mud-brick buildings decay and collapse in the climate of the Near East. New houses are built on top of the remains of the old ones. After many centuries the debris forms a mound, called a *tell*. On the flat Mesopotamian landscape, *tells* are very noticeable.

Using metals and clay

Major changes happened in about 8500 BC. At Chayonu in Anatolia (modern Turkey), over 100 copper beads, pins, and tools have been found. Copper may have come from a local source of ore rather than being smelted. Copper beads have also been discovered in the Zagros Mountains, at Ali Kosh.

At the nearby site of Ganj Dareh, the rectangular buildings were made of long, handmade mud-bricks. Many human and animal figurines (small figures) modeled in clay and pottery vessels have also been found there.

At Mureybet, at the western end of the Fertile Crescent, four lightly fired pots were found in a house. This pottery can be dated to 8000 BC

▷ An early mud-brick, shaped by the brick-maker's hand. He has pressed his thumbs into the top, leaving a herring-bone pattern. This was not decoration, but done to fix the mortar and to let it "breathe."

△ Later, mud-bricks became straight-sided, made from a mixture of mud, chopped straw, and water. The mixture is placed in a mold, then left to dry in the sun for several days.

▷ Mud-bricks are still used in the Near East. Their shape and size have varied from period to period, so bricks can help to date a building. Square bricks were easier to use than other shapes.

and is 500 years older than any other examples. A new industry had begun in the Near East. It signaled a major step in the history of technical development.

Trade

Jericho, an oasis town, may have been a trading center for salt and bitumen from the nearby Dead Sea, cowrie shells from the Red Sea, and turquoise and copper from the Sinai peninsula. All these products were widely traded throughout the Near East. Obsidian was found at Jericho and at other sites as far away as Jarmo in Iraqi Kurdistan. This volcanic glass, with a much sharper cutting edge than flint, comes only from Anatolia.

Traders may have traveled distances of up to 500mi. Because many items, such as textiles and skin products, have not survived, the full extent of the trade network cannot be known.

Clay-using cultures of the Near East
Periods are represented by named archaeological sites.

9000–8500 BC PROTO-NEOLITHIC PERIOD (PRE-POTTERY NEOLITHIC A)
Sites: Jericho, Jordan; Mureybet, Syria

First evidence of handmade bricks

8500–7000 BC ACERAMIC NEOLITHIC PERIOD (PRE-POTTERY NEOLITHIC B)
Sites: Jericho, Jordan; Ain Ghazal, Jordan; Beidha, Jordan; Mureybet, Syria; Tell Abu Hurerya, Syria; Chayonu, Turkey; Jarmo, Iraq; Ganj Dareh, Iran
Use of handmade bricks; rectangular houses with plaster floors; clay modeling of animal and human figurines.

8000 BC
Site: Mureybet, Syria

First evidence of fired pottery

△ Shells were sometimes inlaid in the eye sockets of skulls buried under the floors of houses at Jericho. The skull was separated from the skeleton after the rest of the body had decayed.

△ A pot made from a type of lime plaster called white ware, developed in about 8000 BC. Before people used pottery, containers were made from many different materials.

▷ Raw materials and trade. The Zagros Mountains were rich in minerals and wood. Copper came from Sinai, while Anatolia supplied obsidian, timber, and metals. Mesopotamia had deposits of bitumen but otherwise lacked any resources. Tracing a metal or a stone to its source helps to understand the development of trade.

Scale 1:17 000 000
0   400km
0   300 miles

Resource
◆ Bitumen
Ag Silver
Au Gold
Cu Copper
Fe Iron
Pb Lead
— Cedar
--- Other timber
basalt Other
→ Imported resource

Geology
☐ Ancient shield
☐ Paleozoic rock
☐ Sedimentary rock
☐ Recent sediment
☐ Volcanic outcrop

THE ART OF POTTERY

After 8000 BC people who lived in villages began using pottery throughout the Near East. Complete pottery vessels are sometimes found at archaeological sites, but usually only hundreds of sherds (pottery fragments) are discovered. Pottery was cheap, especially if it was locally produced, so if a vessel broke, it was just thrown away.

Baked clay, from which pottery is made, is almost indestructible and can survive all sorts of weather conditions. Even if a city was burnt, the pottery fragments would survive. Many sites are covered with a layer of potsherds that are left after the wind and rain have washed away the surface soil. These remains help archaeologists learn about a site.

What pottery tells us about a site

Pottery can be used to date a site, especially before the invention of writing. In different periods and at different places, pottery was produced in various ways and decorated with particular designs. From the range of sherds they collect at a site, archaeologists can work out when people lived there.

Similar pottery styles found at a number of sites in a region show that people lived in these places at about the same time. Different types of pottery tell us about changes in the settlement of a region over hundreds or thousands of years. Where imported pottery (brought in by trade) is found, we can sometimes work out the links between different groups of people.

◁ This early, handmade pottery container from about 6500 BC is crudely made and only lightly fired. It is porous and could not be used to store liquids. The herringbone pattern on its surface was made using a sharp tool.

△ Pottery vessels found in an excavation are drawn in crosssection so that archaeologists can compare the pottery types from different sites. The left-hand side shows the outside of the bowl and the right-hand side the inside. The drawing is made to scale and shows any decoration.

◁ Some styles of pottery were decorated to a high artistic standard. The bowl on the left shows four ibexes (mountain goats) arranged in a cross pattern. It dates from about 5000 BC, and the style is called Samarra. The beautiful multicolored plate on the right is from the Halaf period (6000– 5400 BC). This fine pottery was only matched by the much later red-and-black Greek Attic ware.

How pottery was made

Pottery is made basically from clay, often mixed with an ingredient called a temper. Tempers vary from sand or plant matter to hair. Materials that are naturally present in some clays, such as mica (a mineral), often look like tempers that people have added.

Pottery can be made in a number of ways. Early vessels were hand-made. Pottery could also be molded in different types of forms. The potter's wheel was invented in about 4500 BC. Pottery made on a wheel often has recognizable marks that show this.

Firing (oven-baking the pottery hard) is also important. Different temperatures and firing times produce different results. The amount of oxygen in a kiln (pottery oven), can change the color of a vessel from red to black.

The surface areas of the pottery could be treated in different ways. They might be given a thin coat of liquid clay called a slip. After 1500 BC glazes (glass-like finishes) were also used. Patterns and designs might be painted on or incised (marked) into the clay using a stick or another tool. Some pots were polished to a shiny finish, a process called burnishing.

▷ A potter is making a vessel using a series of coils which he will build up, either smoothing them with his hand or finishing them on a potter's wheel. Most pottery was wheel-made, but some vessels were molded. Bowls were made by pressing clay into forms. They were very common and may have been used to bake bread. Nearby are the pots which the potter has made and decorated. Some designs were marked on the surface using a sharp instrument or a stick. Others were painted with vegetable dyes. Finally, the vessels would be fired hard in a pottery kiln (oven).

TOWARD CIVILIZATION (7000–4000 BC)

Pottery use was widespread in the Near East by 7000 BC. Distinctive pottery types emerged at different sites, after which the cultures have been named. Most settlements were in the dry-farming zone of rainfall (10in a year). Over the next 3,000 years village life became more organized, and fields were irrigated.

Hassuna, Samarra, and Choga Mami cultures
The rectangular mud-brick houses at Hassuna, in northern Iraq, had several rooms and court-yards. Pottery was fired in large domed kilns. Clay spindle whorls indicate that wool was woven here. Obsidian, turquoise, and sea-shells found here point to trade with Anatolia and Sinai.

The Samarra and Choga Mami cultures spread south from Hassuna. East at Choga Mami, water channels show that irrigation was practiced. In these areas the rainfall was not enough to grow crops.

▽ Ubaid pottery was decorated with dark painted patterns on a pale background.

▷ An Ubaid female figurine from Ur with a distinctive and unusual "lizard-like" head.

▷ Finely carved jars and a bowl made from alabaster (a compound of gypsum and water). They were found in graves from the Samarran period excavated at Tell al-Sawwan in central Iraq.

▽ Early pottery cultures, 7000–5400 BC. In about 6000 BC the Hassuna culture overlapped the Samarra culture. About 1,000 years later the Halaf culture spread through the Zagros Mountains across to northern Syria. The Ubaid culture developed in Sumer in southern Mesopotamia.

Pottery cultures, 7000–4000 BC
Cultures are represented by named archaeological sites.

7000 BC PROTO-HASSUNA

6800 BC HASSUNA
Sites: Hassuna, Iraq; Tell Umm Dabaghiyeh, Iraq

6500 BC SAMARRA
Sites: Tell al-Sawwan, Iraq; Choga Mami, Iraq

6000 BC HALAF (EARLY)
Sites: Tell Halaf, Syria; Arpachiyeh, Iraq; Yarim Tepe, Iraq

5900 BC UBAID (EARLY)
Site: Tell Halaf, Syria

5400 BC UBAID (LATE)   *Site*: Eridu, Iraq

Halaf culture

The Hassuna culture was replaced by the Halaf, named after the site on the Khabur river in Syria. People here lived in domed mud-brick round huts called *tholoi*. The Halaf culture produced beautifully painted pottery. By 5500 BC the northern Halaf culture came into contact with the Ubaid culture.

Ubaid culture

The Ubaid culture developed in the south of Mesopotamia and lasted for over 1,000 years. At Eridu in Sumer, a series of temples were built, possibly to the water god Enki. A cemetery was found containing 200 rectangular mud-brick graves. The houses had a central room flanked by two rows of rooms. The distinctively painted pottery from the Late Ubaid has been found in Saudi Arabia, Bahrain, and Qatar. This shows that there was already appreciable trade with The Gulf region.

Southern limit of dry farming
Distribution of pottery 7000–5400 BC
- Hassuna
- Samarra
- Halaf
- Early Ubaid

Scale 1: 8 000 000
0 — 200 km
0 — 150 miles

Tell Madhhur

Tell Madhhur is in eastern Iraq not far from the Iranian border. It was excavated as part of a project to study sites that have now been flooded by the construction of a nearby dam.

In the center of the mound was a large house built in about 4000 BC during the Late Ubaid period. The walls of the house, almost 7ft high, had remained standing because, although the house had been burnt, people had deliberately filled it in with soil. Everyday household items such as pottery vessels, clay spindle whorls, and stone hoes had also survived.

▷ A bird's-eye view of the Tell Madhhur house, showing its layout. The hearth where the food was cooked is in the central room. Side rooms were used for storing vegetables and grain. The house was single-story. A ramp led up to the roof, where people may have slept, as they still do today in the Near East during hot summer nights. Several families probably shared the house.

excavated area

Ubaid house

contours at 20 inch intervals

◁ The Tell Madhhur site. Much of the area was buried under thick layers of silt that had been deposited in the valley since Ubaid times. The Ubaid village had about 12 houses, all built in the same tripartite style.

In ancient times many daily tasks were carried out in the same area, and rooms were multi-purpose.

1. *Main living area, with the hearth where food was cooked and bread was baked. In winter people slept here.*

2. *Adjacent kitchen area where people are grinding grain to make bread. Other food preparation also took place.*

▷ A baked-clay pestle shaped like a bent nail. In the Late Ubaid period many tools were made out of baked clay. They were as strong as stone utensils. Other baked-clay items found at Tell Madhhur include grind-stones and spindle whorls.

"Tripartite" architecture

The house had a long central room, the main living area, flanked on each side by several smaller rooms. This was the usual way that Ubaid houses were built. The design is called "tripartite" because the house had three areas (the central room and the two sides). Tripartite houses have been found at Ubaid sites such as Tepe Gawra in northern Iraq.

The style also seems to have been used for temples. Three temples at Tepe Gawra were built according to a tripartite plan, as were others in the south, at Eridu and Uruk. Where this style first came from is not known, but it became the main form for Near Eastern temple architecture. People built tripartite temples for almost 2,000 years, from southern Mesopotamia to northern Syria.

3. *Side storage room where grain is sieved.*

4. *Stairs leading to the roof of the single-story house where people slept in summer.*

5. *Storage rooms for food.*
6. *Entrance to house.*
7. *Open drainage channel.*

△ Not all the tools found at Tell Madhhur were baked clay. These stone hoes were made of chipped flint. They would have been attached to a wooden handle by bitumen and a cord. Only stone and clay products survived the fire.

△ Among the 78 pottery items found in the house was this small painted cup or bowl. Pottery of all shapes and sizes was found. Some of the grain-storage jars were enormous and could hold 24 gallons

△ A spouted jar, for storing and pouring liquids, was found in the kitchen. Similar vessels have been found at other sites. Most pots in the house were hand-made, but some may have been finished on a wheel.

BIRTH OF THE CITY (4000–3000 BC)

The first cities developed in southern Mesopotamia in about 4000 BC. Much earlier, Jericho and Catal Hüyuk had shown some of the features of cities – including walls and closely spaced housing. But these early sites were unique, and the "urban revolution" only began later in the Uruk period.

The change from village to city life took place between 4300 and 3450 BC. Larger numbers of people began living more closely together, and many of them ceased to be farmers. In the Early and Middle Uruk periods, the northern region around Nippur was well populated. In the Late Uruk period, most settlements were in southern Mesopotamia. This movement of people may have been caused by the Euphrates river changing its course. In the following Jamdat Nasr and Early Dynastic periods, many thousands of people lived in the city of Uruk and its surrounding areas.

Specialized labor

Large urban populations involved a very different social organization from that of villages. Many people became specialists in crafts and trades instead of farmers. In the Uruk period, large temples were built. Artistic activity increased throughout the Near East, reaching Egypt in about 3000 BC. Traders were active, importing lapis lazuli, a blue semiprecious stone, over 1,250mi from Afghanistan. Copper and its alloys became common and may have been worked by professional smiths. A metal industry was developing, using gold, silver, copper, lead, and iron.

Farmers were using the ox-plow by 4000 BC, and their produce may have been carried to the cities in carts pulled by oxen or, in the marshes of southern Mesopotamia, by boat. Records made by scribes of the goods received at Uruk are the earliest known written documents.

▷ The Arabs who live in the marshes of southern Iraq today still use boats for transport. The boats are built from reeds, waterproofed with bitumen. They are similar in design to boats found at the Royal Cemetery at Ur (about 2600 BC). Clay models of boats were found in an Ubaid grave at Eridu from about 4000 BC.

▽ Towns of the Late Uruk period. When the Euphrates changed its course, many settlements were abandoned in the north. Large numbers of people moved south, settling nearer Uruk, which was already a big city.

Uruk-based cultures
Cultures are represented by named archaeological sites.
4300–3450 BC
EARLY AND MIDDLE URUK
Sites: Nippur region, Iraq; Uruk, Iraq
3450–3000 BC
LATE URUK
Sites: Uruk, Iraq
3000 BC
JAMDAT NASR
Sites: Uruk, Iraq; Jamdat Nasr, Iraq

▷ Towns of the Early–Middle Uruk period. More than half the population of southern Mesopotamia lived in the fertile alluvial plains to the north and east of and around Nippur. The Euphrates and Tigris rivers were then joined farther upstream.

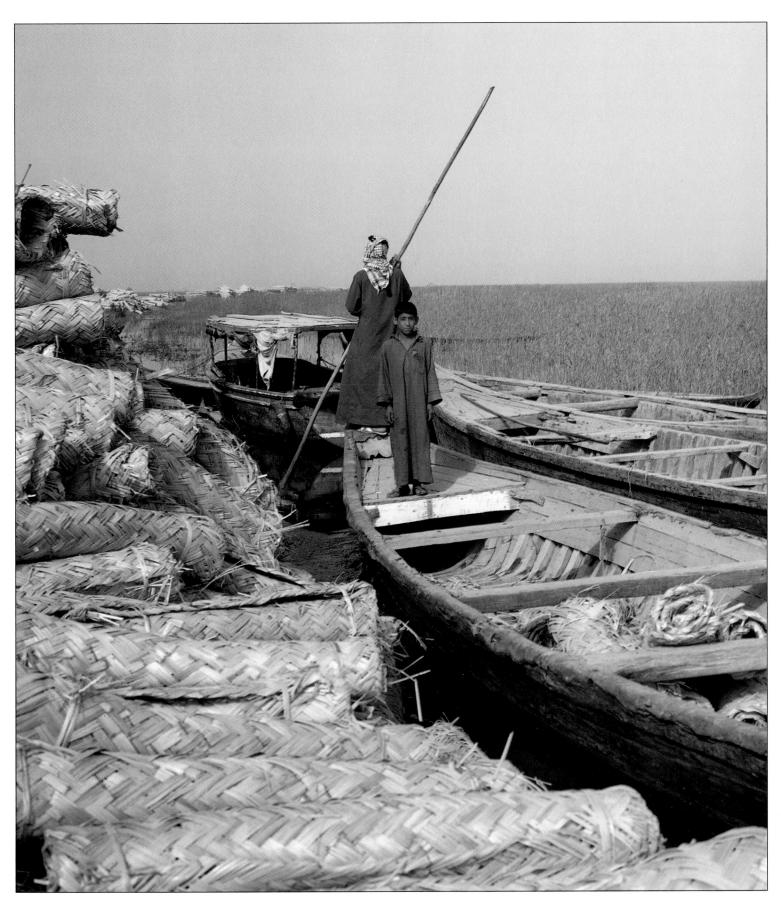

MESOPOTAMIAN SITES

Uruk

Uruk was one of the mightiest cities in Sumer, southern Mesopotamia, between 4000 BC and 3000 BC. The site is near modern Warka, 156mi southeast of Baghdad. The Bible mentions Uruk twice: in Genesis, ch. 10 (as Erech), and in Ezra, ch. 4.

Uruk probably developed from two Ubaid settlements, Kullaba and Eanna, where there were temples to the sky god, Anu, and the goddess of love, Inanna. In about 3000 BC the two sites joined together to form a single city. Uruk covered an area of 1,000 acres and was surrounded by a wall 6mi long.

Gilgamesh, the hero of the great Sumerian story *The Epic of Gilgamesh*, was said to be a king of Uruk.

▷ The Warka vase was one of an alabaster pair found in a temple treasure hoard at Uruk. It dates from at least 3000 BC but is probably older. The vase was valued even in ancient times, for it was repaired with copper rivets holding together broken pieces of the rim. It is now in the Iraq Museum, Baghdad.

▷ A detail from the Warka vase. The goddess Inanna, or her priestess, stands in front of long reed poles (*top center*). She receives a gift from a man in a long gown, perhaps the king of Uruk. The many offerings behind her include two vases like the Warka vase. Two priestly figures stand on the sheep's back.

▷ A priestly procession is entering the temple precinct at Uruk. The mighty columns of the monumental entrance are over 6ft in diameter and are decorated with colored cones stuck into the plaster. A sheep and piles of dates are being brought to the goddess Inanna. The temples were much involved in the way food production was organized.

Temples and their treasures

An important religious site grew up at Uruk, centered on the two temples of Anu and Inanna. The tripartite temples were built on a terrace taking up one-third of the city. Parts of the temple were decorated with geometric designs made from thousands of stone or clay cones painted red, black, and white.

Treasures from the temples were as splendid as the buildings themselves. A white marble woman's face was found in a pit near the Inanna temple. The mask is almost lifesize and probably had semiprecious stones (lapis lazuli) inlaid in the eye sockets. This superb work of art, known as the "Mona Lisa of Uruk," may have represented Inanna herself.

An alabaster vessel over 3ft high was found at the Uruk temple site. The Warka vase, with three bands of carving, shows the earliest known religious scene in Mesopotamia. In the top band, food is being offered to Inanna. In the middle a procession of naked men (possibly priests) carry baskets of produce. The bottom band has a frieze of sheep and grain-heads. The carvings seem to represent a thanksgiving festival for good harvests.

CYLINDER SEALS

Cylinder seals are small cylinder-shaped objects on which a scene or a design is carved. The seal's carving leaves a "print" when it is rolled out on clay. The scene can be reproduced as many times as the cylinder seal is turned. Cylinder seals average about 1in high and ⅔in in diameter. They were usually made out of stone, but metal, ivory, wood, bone, shell, and baked clay were also used. Being small, they were easy to carry.

History of cylinder seals

The earliest cylinder seals to be found are from Uruk and are dated about 3500 BC. The idea spread quickly throughout the Near East and as far as Egypt. Cylinder seals were valuable, especially those made from semiprecious stone, and were probably passed down from one generation to the next. After about 3,000 years, people gradually stopped using the seals because alphabets came into use.

◁▷ A limestone cylinder seal and a drawing of the impression that was made in clay. The metal mount at the top is fashioned as a bull, echoing the cattle design on the seal print.

▽ The *mudhif* or guest-house of the Marsh Arabs of southern Iraq is still built of reeds today. Its ancient design is shown on cylinder seals from Late Uruk times (3000 BC).

▽ Many cylinder seals were made of luxury stones, such as lapis lazuli, and worn by their owners as jewelry. The seals were usually pierced lengthwise so that they could be worn on a pin or a piece of string, or mounted on a swivel.

▽ Cylinder seals were made by cutting hard stone with flint or copper tools. When the cylinder had been shaped, the artist would carve the scene or design. Cylinders were pierced with a hand bore to make the hole through which a pin or wire was threaded.

▷ The man on the left has cut off small lumps of clay, which he is flattening onto pots. He then gives them to the overseer, who rolls a cylinder seal over them to produce a pattern or impression. When they have set, the seals are attached with rope to the necks of the jars.

◁▽ A series of cylinder seal "prints" from different periods. They show animals and mythological creatures. Some of the prints have cuneiform (wedge-shaped writing) inscriptions.

What cylinder seals were used for

Cylinder seals were used to mark the ownership of property. In the case of a storage jar, impressions on a lump of clay would be attached to a string which tied down the cover. Cylinder seals were also used with cuneiform (wedge-shaped) writing, which had also developed at Uruk. Legal and commercial documents were written on clay tablets and often show the impression of a cylinder seal engraved with the owner's name.

The cuneiform inscriptions on cylinder seals tell us the names that people had and about family history. Their carved designs often show scenes from daily life or highlight the role of the king. Many scenes also illustrate the gods, religious worship, and Mesopotamian mythological stories. People may have believed that their seals had magical properties.

The clay impressions left by the seals provide valuable archaeological evidence too. At Jamdat Nasr, north of Uruk, a cylinder-seal print on a clay tablet bore the symbols of the gods of many towns. Similar clay sealings have been found at Ur in Sumer, perhaps suggesting that there was a league of city-states.

WRITING

The earliest known writing comes from Uruk and has been dated to about 3300 BC. It took the form of "word-pictures" drawn with a pointed instrument (a stylus) on to tablets of damp clay. Much later the complete system had more than 700 signs. The tablets measured about 2in wide and were ¾in thick. Each word-picture represented an object: a bull's head meant cattle, an ear of barley meant grain.

Writing developed at Uruk as a convenient way to keep records of produce and accounts of trade. The first tablets that can be read record the transfer of food and other goods including beer. Writing was used first for business – and only much later to record literature and history.

△ Cuneiform signs were made by pressing a sharpened reed stylus into clay (*right*). Most tablets were square, but round ones (*left*) were used for scribes to learn to write on. It took many years to learn the hundreds of signs.

△ A cuneiform letter and its envelope. Clay tablets were often put inside such containers. To make sure nobody changed the contents of the letter, identical writing was put on the outside too.

△ A hollow clay sphere and tokens. The markings on the sphere may show the number and range of tokens once enclosed inside. Many such spheres with tokens have been found in Elam (southwest Iran) and Sumer .

▷ A clay tablet from Uruk inscribed with a very early form of writing. The signs in the lower line may be read as "priest", "prince" and "great". The wedges may be numbers.

Tokens for trade

Tokens had developed much earlier than writing. Clay tokens came in various shapes and sizes, perhaps representing different objects. A cone may have meant a bag of wheat, for example, and a disk, a sheep.

Tokens were placed inside hollow clay spheres (balls) that were then sealed. If one person sent six sheep to another, the sender would put six tokens in the sphere. When the sheep arrived the receiving person would break open the sphere and count the tokens. Then the person would know whether the correct number of sheep had arrived.

The number of tokens also began to be marked on the surface of the sphere. This was probably how writing on clay tablets began.

▷ In the temple warehouse, jars of barley and dates are being stacked by laborers. A temple scribe records amounts of produce on a tablet, while a senior official checks the tablets that are drying on the table. Many early cuneiform documents are lists of food received by temples.

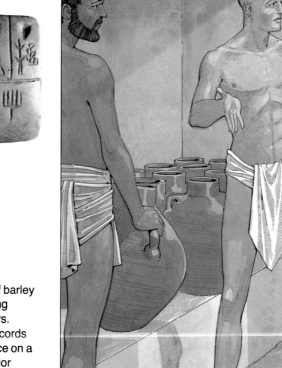

▷ The main stages in the development of the cuneiform script. The later signs have changed greatly from the original word-pictures. This is partly because by 700 BC the signs had been turned 90 degrees (a right angle). The signs went through many changes of both position and meaning. The Assyrians had a vocabulary of 570 signs of which 300 were often used.

PICTOGRAPHIC SIGN c. 3100 BC									
INTERPRETATION	star	?sun over horizon	?stream	ear of barley	bull's head	bowl	head + bowl	lower leg	?shrouded body
CUNEIFORM SIGN c. 2400 BC									
CUNEIFORM SIGN c. 700 BC (turned through 90°)									
PHONETIC VALUE*	dingir, an	u_4, ud	a	še	gu_4	nig_2, ninda	ku_2	du, gin, gub	lu_2
MEANING	god, sky	day, sun	water, seed, son	barley	ox	food, bread	to eat	to walk, to stand	man

* Some signs have more than one phonetic value and some sounds are represented by more than one sign. U_4 means the fourth sign with the phonetic value u.

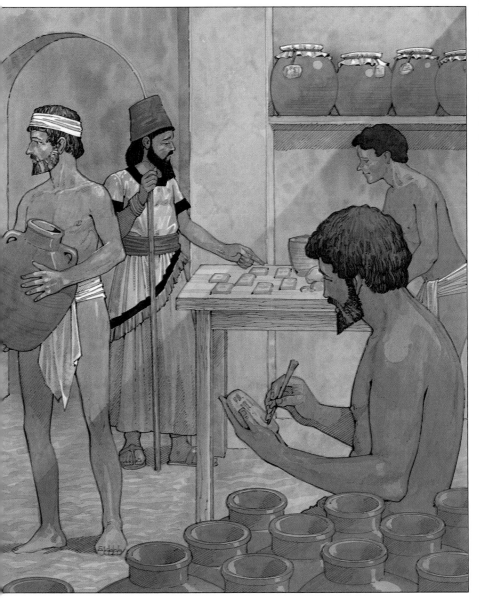

Cuneiform script

The word-pictures written on the tablets at Uruk developed into the script we now call cuneiform. It was a complicated process.

The pictures began to represent ideas and became "ideographs." For example, a bull's head might also mean strength, and the sign of a leg might mean both a person and also "to walk." Later the signs became "phonograms" representing sounds as well as the meaning of a picture. The sign of a bull's head now equaled the sound or syllable (a unit of pronunciation of a word) "gu."

Cuneiform (from the Latin *cuneus* = wedge) was a syllabic script with hundreds of wedge-shaped signs that developed from the original pictures.

Who used cuneiform?

Cuneiform was used by many different peoples during its 3,000-year history. The Sumerians were the earliest to write in cuneiform. The Assyrians adopted the script in about 2300 BC, and it was used by the Babylonians, the Elamites in nearby Iran, the Hittites, the Hurrians, and the Urartu who lived in Anatolia. Cuneiform also appears in the Levant.

Other scripts, such as hieroglyphics (a form of picture-writing), were known in the Near East, but cuneiform was the language of politics until the 5th century BC. It died out in the face of a language that emerged in Syria in about 900 BC: Aramaic – with only 22 letters – was much easier and quicker to write.

STATES IN CONFLICT (3000–2350 BC)

When the Early Dynastic I period replaced the Uruk culture in about 3000 BC, Sumer became a land of city-states. Each state consisted of a city and its lands. There were few physical boundaries in southern Mesopotamia besides the water channels, and city-states fought wars with each other – though they remained mostly independent. The first kings came to power at this time.

The city-state and its priests and leaders

The center of economic wealth in the city-state was the temple. As the home of the patron god or goddess, it was the city's main feature, owned large areas of land and employed many people. The chief priest was called *en* or "lord."

The cities had governors called *ensis*. Decisions were made by the free male citizens, probably those who owned land, in a form of

△ One of more than a dozen known copies of the Sumerian King List. The original, now lost, was written in about 2100 BC.

democracy. There was an upper house of "elders," probably distinguished citizens, and a lower house of "men," perhaps the other landowners.

In times of crisis, the assembly would elect a leader, called a *lugal*. He was the commander in battles with other city-states. He acted as a judge in disputes and later carried out rituals such as blessing the harvests. He lived in a "great house" or *egal*, a word that came to mean palace.

The *lugal* or "great man" began to rival the temple in power and wealth. At some point, the position of leader became permanent. Instead of being elected, the *lugal* became a hereditary king. Kings saw themselves as chosen by a "council of the gods" – which met only at the city of Nippur – to carry out the gods' will.

◁ A stone wall-plaque from Girsu, in present-day Iraq. Ur-Nanshe, the ruler of Lagash (about 2480 BC), one of the Sumerian city-states, is shown carrying a basket of bricks on his head. He is acting in his role as the builder of the city and is watched by a female figure who could be a priestess. In the lower part he is seated on his throne with a cup in his hand. The plaque is inscribed in cuneiform, and the hole indicates that it may have been mounted on a pole.

△ Cities in the Sumerian King List. Southern Mesopotamia was divided into two regions. Sumer in the south stretched from Eridu, which was once on The Gulf, to Nippur. The Sumerian King List listed the names of the rulers of the cities of Sumer and the length of their reigns. Reigns were often listed as being very long, even thousands of years. The King List was written to reinforce the idea that kings were linked closely to the gods, who gave assent to their rule. Although not all the facts it states are true, the King List can help to understand history.

The Early Dynastic period

Sites: Eshnunna (Tell Asmar), Iraq; Tutub (Khafaje), Iraq

3000–2750 BC	EARLY DYNASTIC I
2750–2650 BC	EARLY DYNASTIC II
2650–2350 BC	EARLY DYNASTIC III

Ensis of Lagash (2570–2342 BC)

The *ensis* of Lagash were not included in the Sumerian King List. Unlike kings, they were not said to have received their position from the gods.

c. 2570 BC	En-Hegal
c. 2550 BC	Lugal-sha-engur
2494–2465 BC	Ur-Nanshe
2464–2455 BC	Akurgal
2454–2425 BC	E-ana-tum
2424–2405 BC	En-ana-tuma I
2404–2375 BC	En-temena
2374–2365 BC	En-ana-tuma II
2364–2359 BC	En-entar-zi
2358–2352 BC	Lugal-anda
2351–2342 BC	Uru-ku-gina

The Sumerian King List

The Sumerian King List is an ancient cuneiform record of royal rulers. At least 12 copies have been found in Babylonia and at Susa and Nineveh. It lists all the kings of the Early Dynastic period, many of whom are mentioned in other cuneiform inscriptions. Although the King List places the kings one after the other, they often ruled at the same time at different city-states.

Sumerian influence in the Near East

Sumer was divided into a number of small city-states. Its political influence was weak, but Sumerian culture spread throughout the Near East. Sumerian-style statues were found at Ashur. The city of Mari in eastern Syria had strong links with Mesopotamia. At Ebla, in western Syria, 8,000 clay tablets were found written in a Sumerian cuneiform script.

41

Nippur

Located 100mi south of Baghdad, Nippur is a huge *tell* 66ft high and covering an area of 750 acres. People lived at Nippur for more than 5,000 years, until the 9th century AD. In the Early Dynastic period, the lands of Sumer and Akkad met at this city.

Enlil, the lord of the air, was the main Sumerian god. His temple at Nippur was the most important shrine in Sumer. Sumerians believed that it was at Nippur that the gods met in an assembly to elect kings.

Kings of the Third Dynasty of Ur may have lived at Nippur in about 2000 BC, but the city was never the capital of a dynasty. Rulers of other cities thought that control of Nippur, with its religious importance, gave them the right to rule all of Sumer and Akkad.

The ziggurat at Nippur was built in about 2100 BC by Ur-Nammu, king of Ur. At the top of this vast tiered structure was Enlil's temple, which was called the *ekur* or "mountain house." It became the most important shrine (holy place) in Mesopotamia. Near the ziggurat was the temple of Inanna, the Mesopotamian goddess of love and war.

The remains of the ziggurat are still very visible, and 100 years ago excavators from the University of Pennsylvania built a dig-house on the top of the mound to protect themselves from the local warring Arab tribes. Since then the site has been much excavated, particularly by archaeologists from the University of Chicago.

◁ The site of Nippur, including features from a unique scale drawing of the city on a cuneiform tablet dated about 1300 BC. The tablet shows the temple of Enlil, the city walls, the gates and the main canal. Thousands of cuneiform tablets have been found at Nippur, where there was a famous scribal school. Excavations at the south end of the site have found where the sharp ends of the wall join. In ancient times the Euphrates flowed by the eastern walls, but later the river changed course.

Map legend:

0 100 200 300 m
0 500 1000 ft

- city wall on tablet
- city gate on tablet
- waterways on tablet
- excavated area

Temple cuneiform labels on tablet

contours at 13ft intervals

Map labels: Nunbirdu Canal, Exalted Temple, ditch, Nergal Gate, North Temple, Gate of the Ritually Impure Women, Exalted Gate, Euphrates River, Nippur, Area WA, Canal in the city, Temple of Enlil, Temple of Enlil, Inanna Temple, Ziggurat, Temple Ekiur, Ekur, Gula Gate, Enclosure of Annigina, Area WB, Shatt al-Nil, garden in the city, Nanna Gate, Uruk Gate, Tablet Hill, TA, TB, Gate facing Ur, ditch, Area WC

Ebla

Tell Mardikh was identified as the ancient city of Ebla in 1968. Located in Syria, south of Aleppo, people lived at Ebla for over 3,500 years, until AD 800. Its most important period was from 2500 BC to 1500 BC.

The Ebla texts

Eight thousand cuneiform texts were discovered at Ebla. They came from the library of what is called "Palace G." Most of the clay tablets were written in Eblaite, a previously unknown local language that is closely related to the language of Akkad. Many of the texts discuss administrative matters. The king was extremely wealthy, owning 80,000 sheep and receiving income of 11lb of gold and 1,100lb of silver each year.

▷ A human-headed golden bull with a stone beard, found in Palace G at Ebla. The figure may be linked to worship of the sun god Shamash. It is Sumerian in style. Later, huge human-headed bulls guarded the entrances to Assyrian places.

▽ A gold necklace, dated to about 1750 BC, found in a tomb beneath Ebla's Western Palace. The decoration on the disks was made with tiny gold granules, and the three-section band was made by "coiling." These techniques were developed in Sumer.

◁▽ *Left*: Ebla's archive room as it was found by the excavators of Palace G. The clay tablets lie where they fell when the wooden shelves collapsed in the city's destruction. Many of the tablets were badly smashed and must be painstakingly pieced together. From traces left behind after the burning of this room, the original shelving system can be worked out (as shown *below)*.

Ebla and Sumer

Ebla had many links with Sumer. Some texts were written in both Eblaite and Sumerian. Delicate gold jewelry found in Palace G had been made using techniques developed in Sumer's Early Dynastic period. A limestone inlay was decorated with battle scenes in typical Sumerian style.

Ebla was a thriving kingdom, at its wealthiest between 2400 BC and 2250 BC, when the Early Dynastic period ended and the Akkadian rulers came to power. Ebla traded far and wide – from nearby Carchemish to central Anatolia, Ashur in northern Mesopotamia, and Afghanistan. After being attacked by the Mesopotamian king Naram-Sin (2254–2218 BC) the city never recovered its economic prosperity.

MESOPOTAMIAN SITES

Ur

The ancient city of Ur is in southern Iraq. It was founded during the Ubaid period in about 4000 BC when people also first settled in Sumer. Ur was near the Euphrates river, and some of the city's earliest remains were covered with heavy silt from it. This may be evidence of a terrible flood, memories of which were handed down and recorded in the Bible (Genesis, chs 6–8).

Genesis, ch. 11, claimed Ur as the home of the Hebrew patriarch Abraham. Ur was also a port for trade with The Gulf until 1700 BC. The main temple was dedicated to the moon god Nanna. The city was abandoned in about 300 BC, probably due to floods.

△ Two lyres as they were found in the tomb of Queen Puabi. In the dust can be seen the cow's head made of gold and lapis lazuli that was attached to one of these musical instruments.

◁ The sacred enclosure with the temple and the ziggurat of Nanna, the moon god. It was built by the kings of the Third Dynasty of Ur (2112–2004 BC). Ur-Nammu, Shulgi, and Amar-Sin also seem to have lived and been buried here. The royal tombs were inside the walls.

▽ Gaming boards similar to this one were found in the royal tombs. They were made from pieces of shell, bone, lapis lazuli, and red limestone set into various patterns. Two sets of seven counters were used to play the game, but the exact rules are unknown.

△ An exquisitely worked gold dagger (with lapis lazuli handle) and sheath. The Sumerian goldsmiths were masters of their craft. The sheath was decorated in fine granules of gold.

The royal cemetery at Ur

Excavations in the 1920s uncovered more than 1,000 graves at Ur from the end of the Early Dynastic period (2600–2400 BC). In some of the tombs spectacular treasures were found, including the so-called "Standard of Ur," a delicately inlaid box with a banquet scene on one side and a war procession on the other. It is now in the British Museum.

Inscriptions identify the royal graves of King Meskalamdug and Queens Puabi and Ninbanda. Mass burials suggest that human sacrifice took place – some kings and queens were buried with their servants, who seem to have died by drinking poison or taking a drug.

△ Reconstructed wooden sledge from the royal tomb of Queen Puabi. Two oxen were found still attached to the sledge in the tomb. The reins passed through a silver ring decorated with a donkey made from electrum (a gold/silver alloy).

△ A stone weight shaped like a duck, found at Ur. The inscription gives its weight as "5 *minas* for Nanna." A *mina* weighed about 1 lb.

▷ A superb electrum helmet from the tomb of King Meskalamdug. The Sumerians could dissolve silver from the surface of the alloy so that it would look like gold. The finely fashioned hair is held in place by a diadem suggesting a royal owner.

ZIGGURATS

Looking very impressive against the flat Mesopotamian landscape, pyramid-shaped ziggurats symbolized sacred mountains and were first built in about 2000 BC. People had already built temples on platforms at Eridu in the Ubaid period, and ziggurats were similar religious buildings. They appeared with the revival of Sumerian rule after the dynasty of Akkad (2334–2154 BC). King Ur-Nammu of the Third Dynasty of Ur constructed ziggurats at Ur, Eridu, Uruk, and Nippur.

Design of the ziggurat at Ur

The ziggurat at Ur had a rectangular base with three staircases that met at right angles and went up to two more stages to reach the high temple. The ziggurat core was made of mudbricks, but burned bricks with a bitumen mortar were used for the outside. Many bricks were stamped with Ur-Nammu's name. Drains carried off the water from the upper parts.

◁ The ziggurat at Tell al-Rimah was built by Shamshi-Adad I in about 1800 BC. The ziggurat was part of the temple building, and the upper shrine was probably reached from the roof of the courtyard temple.

The ziggurat of Babylon

Ziggurats were built throughout southern and northern Mesopotamia and also in Elam. When Babylon became the center of religious worship, its ziggurat became more famous than the one at Ur. It stood for 1,000 years until Sennacherib demolished it in 689 BC. Dedicated to the god Marduk, the ziggurat became identified with the biblical tower of Babel (Genesis, ch. 11).

Herodotus, the Greek historian, described the ziggurat at Babylon as having six levels crowned by a temple. Its dimensions were also given in a Babylonian clay tablet. The ziggurat was called Etemenanki, which means "the temple of the foundation of heaven and earth."

▽ Building a ziggurat involved hundreds of laborers. Some carry mud-bricks, which are being made nearby. These will be used to build the upper stages of the ziggurat. Other laborers carry reeds that will be woven into matting to be placed between the layers of bricks.

▲ Possible ziggurat

Period of initial ziggurat construction
- ▲ Ur III (2100–2000 BC)
- △ Old Babylonian (1900–1700 BC)
- ▲ Elamite, Kassite, Middle Assyrian (1400–1100 BC)
- ▲ Late Assyrian (900–600 BC)

- - - - Ancient coastline
———— Ancient course of river

Scale 1: 8 300 000
0   200 km
0   150 miles

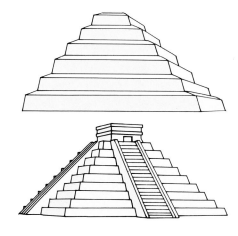

△ Ziggurats of Mesopotamia. Ziggurats have been excavated at 16 sites. Others are known from the shape of the mound or from literature. Dur-Sharrukin was one of the first excavated.

▽ Ziggurats look like the stepped pyramids in Egypt (*top*), which were tombs. Stepped temples are found in Central America (*bottom*), but there was no contact with Mesopotamia.

47

RELIGION AND RITUAL

According to Mesopotamian religion, human beings were created to serve the gods. Each city had a patron god, and these gods lived in images in the temples dedicated to them. The priests and other people who worked at the temples were their servants. Kings were thought to be appointed by the will of the gods.

Mesopotamian gods

Anu, the sky god, was the chief Sumerian god. His city was Uruk, which also housed the famous Eanna temple complex of Inanna, goddess of love and war. Enlil, the "lord of the wind," whose city was Nippur, was the son of Anu. He replaced his father as the main god. Enki, god of living water, had his temple at Eridu. Ur was the city of Nanna, the moon god. Temples at Larsa and Sippar were built for the sun god Utu.

By 2000 BC, the Sumerian gods became combined with the Akkadian gods and took their names. Inanna became Ishtar. Shamash, which literally meant "sun," replaced Utu. Nanna was now called Sin. In Babylonian times, Marduk became the chief god, with his temple at Babylon.

△ Priests slaughtering a ram. Animal sacrifices were common and could involve large numbers of sheep. The intestines would be examined for omens about the future.

▷ Drawings of seal impressions in clay, found at Ashur. The dog was the symbol of the goddess Gula. The goat-fish was linked with Ea, god of waters.

◁ A group of Sumerian statues from Eshnunna. They are not gods but represent worshipers and were placed in the temples to pray for the life of the person who gave them. The hands are clasped in prayer. Some of the eyes, inlaid with bitumen and shell, are still intact. Each person was believed to have a special god or goddess who would protect them from demons.

Images of the gods, spirits, and demons

The Mesopotamians thought that their gods looked and behaved like people, though they had supernatural powers. Cylinder seals and other pieces of art show gods and goddesses with human bodies. The gods were shown with beards. To signal that they were different from people, images of the gods and goddesses always included a distinctive multi-tiered horned crown or helmet and a seven-petaled rosette engraved near the head.

Gods and goddesses also had their own symbols. The crescent and circle represented Sin, the moon god. The star was Ishtar's sign. Sometimes the gods held their symbols in their hands. At other times the divine symbols sprouted from their shoulders. The images of the gods and goddesses often changed throughout Mesopotamian history.

Besides the gods, people in the Near East believed in supernatural spirits and demons, both good and bad. Many of these took half-human and half-animal forms. Some demons were thought to cause diseases and other misfortunes, which superstitious people took complicated precautions to avoid.

▷ A bronze statue of the king of the evil wind demons, Pazuzu. He is shown with grotesque face, four wings, bird's legs, animal paws and a scorpion's tail. Demons such as Pazuzu were not always evil and sometimes protected people from other demons!

△ King Ur-Nammu (2112–2095 BC) makes a libation (drink offering) to the moon god Sin. Sin is seated on a throne, holding in his hand a rod, a ring and possibly a necklace. Water, beer, oil, wine, and blood were used for libations.

PART TWO

KINGDOMS AND EMPIRES

△ A cuneiform tablet from the royal library at Nineveh, recording observations of the stars and planets. Assyrian kings employed expert astrologers.

▷ Detail from the "war" side of the "Standard of Ur," found in the Royal Cemetery at Ur. It shows the victorious troops of Ur, on foot or in chariots. Four mules pull the empty chariot (*top left*) of the king (*top right*) who holds a mace in his hand as a symbol of kingship.

KINGS OF AGADE (2350–2000 BC)

Mesopotamia became united when Sargon of Akkad conquered both the northern and southern regions of Mesopotamia. The Akkadian language was now spoken rather than Sumerian, and Mesopotamian rule extended throughout the Near East.

Sargon of Agade

Sargon was the first king of the dynasty of Agade and ruled for 56 years. His name in Akkadian meant "the true king," but his origins were humble. The Sumerian King List states that his father was a date-grower, and another account says that he was a gardener favored by the goddess Ishtar.

Sargon built a new capital city at Agade, probably near Babylon. He conquered the city-states of Uruk, Ur, Umma, and Lagash in southern Mesopotamia, and he was also called the King of Kish and King of the Land.

▽ The kings of Agade conquered an empire that stretched from the Mediterranean to modern Iran. Sargon claimed that he ruled the whole world "from the sunrise to the sunset." This boast could have been a later tradition. From their widespread territories, the kings of Agade obtained such raw materials as wood from Lebanon and silver from Anatolia.

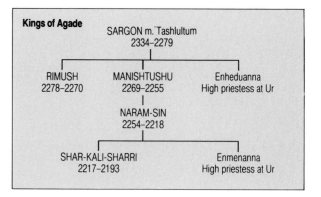

Sargon's sons

Rimush and Manishtushu, Sargon's sons, continued their father's military campaigns. They took Akkadian rule as far north as Ashur and Nineveh and also east into the Elamite territories. Talking about his conquests of the distant regions Anshan and Sherihum, now in Iran, Manishtushu said: "It is absolutely true!"

△ A limestone statue of Gudea, the ruler of Lagash, who wears a fur headdress. He is holding a vase from which flow two streams of living water, symbolized by the fish.

▽ This superb life-size head was made from copper. It is hollow, but the eyes would have been inlaid with stones. The beard, hair, and diadem indicate a king, possibly Sargon or Naram-Sin.

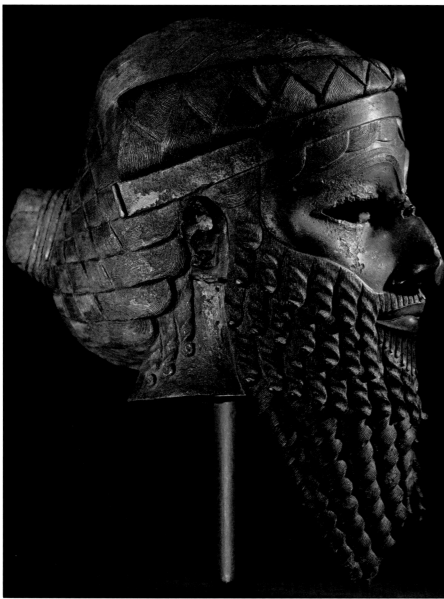

Naram-Sin

Naram-Sin, Sargon's grandson, ruled for 37 years and called himself King of the Universe. His empire extended from Susa in the east to Ebla on the Mediterranean coast. He claimed to be a god, making people address him as "god of Agade," and inscriptions show his name marked with the sign that was used to indicate gods. Naram-Sin was followed by his son, Shar-kali-sharri, who reigned for 17 years. But the empire of Agade began to collapse because of internal problems and pressure from the Gutians, who came from the Zagros Mountains. The city of Agade was sacked and has never been found.

The Third Dynasty of Ur

With the downfall of the Akkadian empire, Sumerian rule revived once more. At Ur, King Ur-Nammu built the famous ziggurat as well as other temples and a palace. Ur-Nammu's power was concentrated in southern Mesopotamia, for he also controlled Eridu and Uruk and erected buildings at Nippur and Larsa. One of his sons married a daughter of the king of Mari, linking the two nations.

Shulgi, Ur-Nammu's son, reigned for 47 years after his father's death. Like Naram-Sin he also claimed he was a god. Shulgi carried on the building work begun by his father and expanded the kingdom eastwards and northwards to Ashur and Susa. He introduced many reforms during his reign, making the governors (*ensis*) and military commanders (*shagins*) report directly to him. Shulgi controlled the temple lands, imposed new taxes, reorganized the system of weights, introduced a new calendar, and established a code of law.

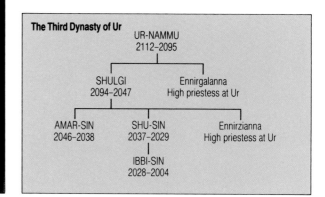

The Third Dynasty of Ur

UR-NAMMU
2112–2095

SHULGI
2094–2047

Ennirgalanna
High priestess at Ur

AMAR-SIN
2046–2038

SHU-SIN
2037–2029

Ennirzianna
High priestess at Ur

IBBI-SIN
2028–2004

RIVAL KINGDOMS (2000–1600 BC)

In about 2000 BC the Third Dynasty of Ur broke up into several smaller kingdoms. This marked the end of a united Mesopotamia. The two most important new kingdoms were Isin and Larsa, after which this period in Mesopotamian history has been named. The most famous king was Rim-Sin of Larsa, who reigned from 1822 BC to 1763 BC. In 1804 BC he defeated Uruk and 10 years later he captured Isin.

New peoples arrived in Mesopotamia and settled among the Akkadian and Sumerian communities. The Amorites – nomads from the Arabian desert region who spoke a Semitic language – became powerful in the kingdoms of Babylon, Kish, and Larsa.

Large numbers of Hurrians, who spoke an Indo-European language, came from Anatolia into northern Mesopotamia and western Syria. Texts from Alalakh on the Orontes river in Syria show that almost half the population there had Hurrian names.

Kingdoms of Mesopotamia, 2025–1595 BC
Selected outstanding kings are listed for each kingdom.

First Dynasty of Isin, 2017–1794 BC
Isme-Dagan (1953–1935 BC)
Lipit-Ishtar (1934–1924 BC)

Larsa Dynasty, 2025–1763 BC
Rim-Sin I (1822–1763 BC)

1763 BC   Rim Sin I defeated by Hammurabi, ending the Larsa dynasty

First Dynasty of Babylon, 1894–1595 BC
Hammurabi (1792–1750 BC)

Asur
Shamshi-Adad I (c. 1813–1781 BC)
Ishme-Dagan I (1780–1741 BC)

Mari
Zimri-Lim (1779–1757 BC)

1757 BC   Zimri-Lim defeated by Hammurabi, and the kingdom of Mari ends

▽ City-states of the Isin and Larsa period. The rival states that followed the Third Dynasty of Ur were often at war with each other. In 1936 BC (*left*) Isin was the largest, stretching from The Gulf to Babylon. Twenty-six years later, in 1910 BC, it included only Nippur. The southern cities of Ur and Eridu were still ruled by Larsa in 1802 BC (*right*), while in the north Babylon had become a major kingdom.

Trade in the south

The southern Mesopotamian kingdoms competed for the rich trade with The Gulf and beyond. They exported silver, oils, textiles, and barley in exchange for copper, gold, ivory, lapis lazuli, pearls, and other goods. Copper was imported from Magan (modern Oman). Beads found in Mesopotamia show links with the Harappan culture of the Indus valley (Pakistan). Many goods were shipped through Dilmun (probably present-day Bahrain).

◁ A lapis lazuli necklace from a tomb in Kish. The blue semiprecious stone was mined in Afghanistan. The long brown carnelian beads are typical of the Harappan culture of the Indus valley. These semiprecious stones were imported.

▽ A donkey caravan at the *karum* (merchant suburb) outside Kanesh, an important trade center in Anatolia. Donkeys have arrived from Ashur, bringing textiles and tin from Iran. Other donkeys will continue farther west and are being loaded up. One of the merchants is watching his scribe count the goods.

Trade and conquest in the north

The kingdoms of northern Mesopotamia also traded. Ashur, on the river Tigris, was an important center with a large merchant colony dealing in wool, textiles and tin. Tin was used to make bronze, instead of copper, for weapons and other goods. It was mined in Iran and Afghanistan and transported by donkey caravans to Kanesh in central Turkey.

Shamshi-Adad, an Amorite, captured many of the northern kingdoms, including Ashur. His lands stretched from the Zagros Mountains to Mari, on the Euphrates (now in Syria). He claimed to have set up a stele or pillar inscribed with his name "in the country of Laban" (that is, Lebanon). After his death, Shamshi-Adad's empire split into several kingdoms. In some places the old kings were restored. In Mari, Zimri-Lim returned to his throne until 1757 BC, when he was conquered by Hammurabi, king of Babylon.

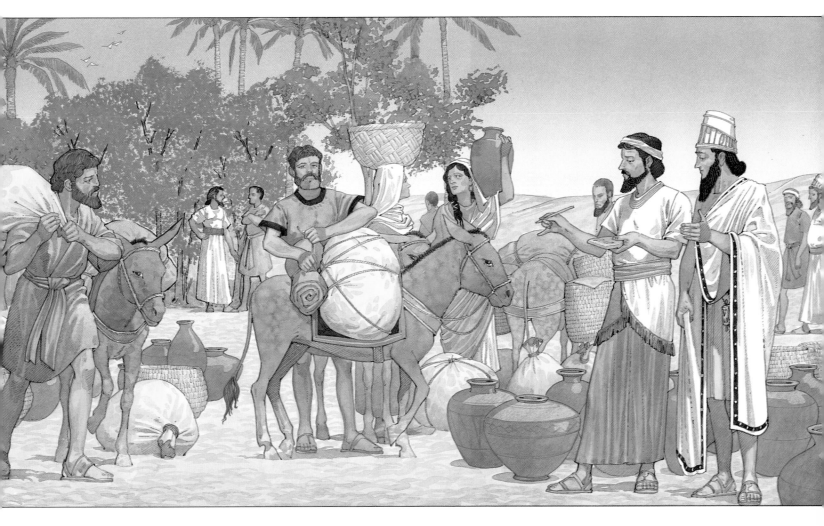

LAW AND SOCIETY

Mesopotamian kings were very concerned to rule justly. Ur-Nammu of Ur (2112–2095 BC) wrote the first known law code in the world. His son, Shulgi of Ur, also produced a law code, as did Lipit-Ishtar of Isin and Dadusha of Eshnunna. The most famous code to have survived is that of King Hammurabi, who ruled Babylon from 1792 BC to 1750 BC.

Hammurabi's law code

Hammurabi's law code is carved on a basalt stele 7½ft high. The opening words record the king's wish "to cause justice to prevail in the land, to destroy the wicked and the evil, that the strong may not oppress the weak."

The law code may not have been used in courts to decide cases, but the 282 sections cover many subjects, especially property and commercial law. If one person wronged another, financial compensation – in the form of a sum of silver – was often paid, as had been the custom in Sumerian law.

The idea of punishment found in the Old Testament – "Life for life, eye for eye, tooth for tooth, hand for hand, foot for foot" (Deuteronomy, ch. 19, verse 21) – also occurs in Hammurabi's code.

◁ This statue, made from diorite, a hard black stone, is thought to be of Hammurabi. He is shown on his law code stele wearing a similar type of headdress. Babylonian kings between 2100 BC and 1700 BC wore the same type of royal apparel. The statue was found at Susa, in modern Iran, where it had been taken as war booty in the 12th century BC.

◁ Hammurabi's kingdom. Hammurabi ruled over Mesopotamia only in the second part of his long reign (1792–1750 BC). He captured Isin and Uruk in 1787 BC. Later, in 1763 BC, with the help of the kings of Mari and Eshnunna, he conquered his long-standing rival, Rim-Sin I of Larsa. In 1761 BC Hammurabi defeated Mari and in 1755 BC he was victorious over Eshnunna.

Babylonian society

Hammurabi's law code divides Babylonian society into three social classes: *awilum* (the Akkadian word meaning "man"), *mushkenum* and *wardum*. The *awilum* were "freemen" who may have been landowners. The *mushkenum* could speak in the assembly of "freemen" but probably did not own property. The *wardum* were slaves. All three classes were, of course, ruled by the king.

When an *awilum* died, his property was divided between his sons. If he fell into debt or could not pay his taxes to the king, he might sell himself, his wife, or his children as slaves.

The king used slaves to build roads, dig canals, and perform other duties. Slaves were expensive to buy, so few were privately owned. Most farms were worked by tenants, who gave a portion of their harvest to the landowner in return for food, animals, and other daily requirements.

Penalties under Hammurabi's code

Hammurabi's law code applied different penalties for the same crime, depending on the social class of the person involved. If the victim was an *awilum*, the person responsible was punished in the same way as they had hurt the victim. Law 196 stated that "If an *awilum* has put out the eye of a *mar-awilum* (the son of an *awilum*), they shall put out his eye". (This was "retributive punishment.")

If the victim was either a *mushkenum* or a *wardum*, then a sum of money would be paid instead. Law 198 states: "If an *awilum* has put out the eye of a *mushkenum* or broken his bone, he shall pay one *mina* of silver".

The idea of retribution – "an eye for an eye" – was not found in Sumerian law and was probably introduced into Mesopotamia by the Amorites.

▷ The stele of Hammurabi's law code from about 1760 BC. The upper part of the basalt pillar shows the king in prayer before the seated Shamash, the sun god and god of justice. Shamash is winged and is also wearing the divine horned crown. He is holding in his right hand a ray of sunlight. The lower part of the stele is inscribed in cuneiform with Hammurabi's 282 laws carved in 49 vertical columns. The Elamites took the stele to Susa in 1159 BC as war booty from Babylon.

MITTANI AND THE RISE OF THE ASSYRIANS

In northern Mesopotamia and the Levant, the kingdom of Mittani became the major power by about 1500 BC. The people of Mittani were Hurrians. (The Hurrian language was very different from other Near Eastern tongues.) Their rulers had Indo-European connections and worshiped ancient Indian gods. The Mittanians used a new military weapon: the horse-drawn two-wheeled chariot. Washukanni, their capital city, was probably in present-day northern Syria.

Warfare with Egypt

Egypt was united by Ahmose, the founder of the 18th dynasty. In this New Kingdom period Egyptian pharaohs conquered much of the Levant and Palestine, with many sites showing signs of massive destruction. Pharaoh Amenophis II (1427–1401 BC) led an army into Mittanian territory, capturing the city of Qadesh on the Orontes river.

▽ The empire of Mittani in about 1500 BC. The empire stretched east from Assyria to the Levant. Washukanni, the capital city, has not been positively identified, but may be Tell al-Fakhariyeh in northern Syria. The region around the upper part of the Habur river was the heartland of the empire. Mittanian documents have also been found nearby at Tell Brak.

The Amarna letters

The only written information about the Mittanians comes from foreign sources. The Amarna letters, a collection of 350 clay tablets, give many details about the government of the Egyptian New Kingdom's territories. They also record diplomatic exchanges between the pharaohs of Egypt and the rulers of independent countries, including Mittani.

Treaties between different states were often cemented through marriage between the rulers' families, and there were many foreign princesses in the harems of the pharaohs. Documents show that royal marriage negotiations were often very complicated and drawn-out. Tuthmosis IV (1401–1391 BC) asked the king of Mittani, Artatama, no less than seven times for the hand of his daughter before his wish was granted. This marriage was probably made in an attempt to block the growing power of the Hittites and the Assyrians.

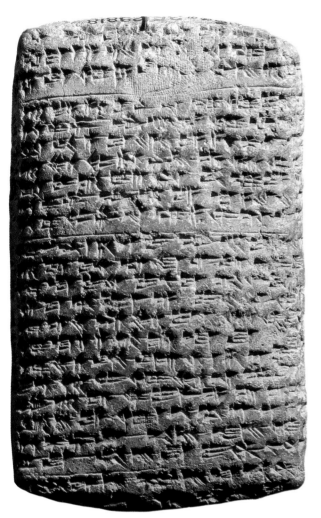

△ One of the 350 letters from Tell Amarna in central Egypt which record the political history of the pharaohs Amenophis III and Akhenaten. These clay tablets were written in cuneiform, using Akkadian, the international language of the time. Many of the letters describe the situation in Palestine. In the letter shown here, the ruler of Amurru explains why he did not receive the pharaoh's envoy in person.

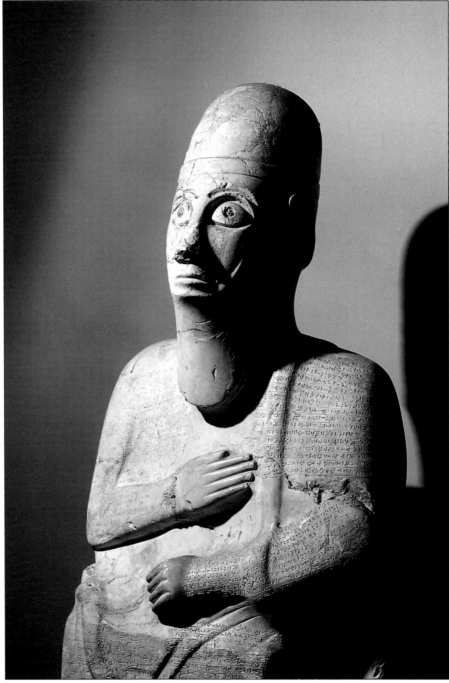

The Hittites and Assyrians

Hattusas in Anatolia was the capital of the Hittites. The Hittites were rivals of the Mittanians for control of their lands, and they ended Hammurabi's dynasty when Mursilis I (1626–1595 BC) overran Babylon.

The Hittites had peaceful relations with the Egyptian pharaohs. Their king Suppiluliumas I made an alliance with the Assyrian powers and married his daughter to the king of Babylon. His victories in Anatolia, the Levant, and northern Mesopotamia reduced the lands held by Mittani, which had grown weaker.

The Assyrian king Adad-nirari (1305–1274 BC) captured Washukanni and made its ruler, Shattuara, his vassal (junior ruler). The Mittanian kingdom came to an end when it was annexed by Adad-nirari's son Shalmaneser I (1273–1244 BC). The Assyrians and the Hittites were now the main powers in Mesopotamia.

△ A statue of king Idrimi of Alalakh, in northern Syria, who was a vassal of the Mittanian rulers. The seated king's hand on his breast shows his allegiance. Details about his life are given in a cuneiform inscription covering most of his body.

THE KASSITE EMPIRE (1600–1200 BC)

The Babylonian King List records that there were 36 Kassite kings of Babylon, covering a period of several hundred years. After the Hittites conquered the city in 1595 BC, Babylon was governed by the Kassites for four centuries, from the end of the 15th until the 12th century BC. The Kassites may have come originally from Central Asia. They did not speak a Semitic language, and only 48 Kassite words have been identified. Some of these are technical terms for horses – and the Kassites were also noted for their horsemanship. When the Kassites first arrived in Babylon they were agricultural workers. Later, even when their kings ruled Babylon, the Kassites do not appear to have been a large group.

Dur-Kurigalzu

The Kassites rebuilt and restored temples at Ur, Uruk, and Isin. But the best-preserved example of their work is at the site of Agar Quf, near Baghdad, which was called Dur-Kurigalzu. This site was a city built to defend the kingdom against Assyria and Elam. There was a palace as well as a ziggurat which still stands today at a height of 188ft. Dur-Kurigalzu was a major city, but the Kassites regarded Babylon as the capital of their empire and also its religious and commercial center.

Kassite Kings	
Kara-indash	c.1415
Kadashman-Harbe 1	
Kurigalzu I	
Kadashman-Enlil I	1374–1360
Burna-Buriash II	1359–1333
Kara-hardash	1333
Nazi-bugash	1333
Kurigalzu II	1332–1308
Nazi-maruttash	1307–1282
Kadashman-Turgu	1281–1264
Kadashman-Enlil II	1263–1255
Kudur-Enlil	1254–1246
Shagarakti-shuriash	1245–1233
Kashtiliash IV	1232–1225
Tulkulti-Ninurta	1224–1216
Enlil-nadin-shumi	1224
Kadashman-Harbe II	1223–1222
Adad-shuma-iddina	1221–1216
Adad-shuma-usur	1215–1186
Melishipak	1185–1171
Marduk-apla-iddina I	1170–1158
Zababa-shuma-iddina	1157
Enlil-nadin-ahi	1156–1154

The Kassite dynasty, c.1570–1154 BC
Selected Kassite kings. (Other rulers from the same period are shown in parentheses.)

c.1570 BC	Agum II
c.1510 BC	Burna- Buriash I
c.1390 BC	Kurigalzu I (Amenophis III of Egypt)
1359–1333BC	Burna-Buriash II
1332–1308 BC	Kurigalzu II (Akhenaten of Egypt)
1263–1255 BC	Kadashman-Enlil II (Hattusilis III, Hittite king)
1232–1225 BC	Kashtiliash IV

Assyrian king Tukulti-Ninurta sacks Babylon

1170–1158 BC	Marduk-apla-iddina
1156–1154 BC	Enlil-nadin-ahi

▽ The Kassite kingdom in the 13th century BC. This was an empire that covered most of southern Mesopotamia. It bordered Elam in the east, (now modern Iran) and the Assyrian territories in the north. The Elamites overran the Kassite kingdom in the mid-12th century BC. They took back some of the war booty from Babylon, including Hammurabi's law code stele and Naram-Sin's victory stele, to their capital city Susa. The booty was discovered there in the 19th century by a French expedition.

△ Made of limestone, this *kudurru* or boundary stone is beautifully carved. The cuneiform inscription records a grant of land.

▷ The ziggurat of Dur-Kurigalzu. European travelers thought that the ziggurat was the Tower of Babel. The reed matting that was laid between every seven layers of brick can still be seen. The bottom platform is a modern restoration.

▽ This painted pottery head, found at Dur-Kurigalzu, shows the realism of Kassite art. The man's face is painted with red ochre, and his beard and other features are in black.

Kassite art and culture

The Kassites kept the Babylonian way of life, even rebuilding the temples of the Mesopotamian gods who were different from theirs. Their art was lively and realistic, especially when depicting animals. Their scribes left thousands of documents written on tablets.

They were the first people in the Near East to make molded baked bricks to form decorative wall friezes. At the Inanna temple at Uruk, the outer wall shows the gods as humans. Molded baked bricks were used 1,000 years later in the palaces built by Nebuchadrezzar at Babylon and Darius at Susa.

The Kassites also showed skill in carving stone. Boundary stones (*kudurru*) were set up to proclaim when land was given by royal grants. They were often richly decorated with images of beasts symbolizing the gods who were believed to witness such grants.

Kassite kings

Several Kassite kings are named in the Amarna letters. Burna-Buriash II (1359–1333 BC) is recorded as complaining that the Egyptian delegation who came to collect his daughter and take her to Egypt to be married had only five carriages – not enough for a princess of high rank! The Amarna letters detail the many gifts exchanged between the Kassite king and the Egyptian pharaoh. The Kassite king Kurigalzu I (about 1390) received gold from Egypt.

The most famous king was Kurigalzu II (1332–1308 BC), who was a successful military leader. He attacked the Elamites and captured Susa, their capital city. Later the tables were turned when the Elamite king Shutruk-Nahhunte attacked the Kassite kingdom. Babylon, the capital, was destroyed and much booty was taken back to Susa. The Kassite period ended in 1154 BC.

EVERYDAY LIFE

By 2000 BC most people in the Near East lived in towns and cities that were protected by walls. Houses were made of mud-brick and had two stories with flat roofs. The doors and windows were made from reeds set in wooden frames. The streets were narrow and winding, like the old parts of cities in the region today.

Food and drink

Barley was used for bread-flour and for beer-making. Beer was also brewed from dates, which were an important source of sugar, as honey was rare. Of beer it was said, "it makes the liver happy and fills the heart with joy." People grew onions, garlic, figs, and pomegranates. Mustard, cress, cumin, and coriander were used. Sheep, goats, and pigs provided meat, and people also ate ducks and geese. There were many different types of fish. Locusts were considered a delicacy.

Clothing and textiles

Cloth was made from the fleece of sheep, which was spun on hand-spindles. Spinning and weaving were done mainly by women, in the house, as a source of household income. Hides of animals were tanned to make leather goods such as bags and sandals. Men and women used both soap and cosmetics. They painted the skin around their eyes with kohl, a metal-based black paint.

Town crafts

There were many different occupations in the towns. Potters produced a wide range of household items, from plates and cups to large containers for storing grain. Carpenters made wooden furniture and tools, though these were also made from copper, tin, and bronze. Other craft workers manufactured metal and glass objects, but these were luxury items.

▷ This 4½in-high sieve pot may have been used to strain the grains when pouring beer, a very popular drink. Pottery items made in a wide variety of shapes and sizes are the most commonly found objects of ancient daily life.

▷ A Near Eastern street market. In the shadow of the ziggurat, traders sell their wares from small booths. The jars hold imported olive oil and wine, while dates and a variety of spices are also on sale. A temple official checks the quality of the food being sold. As coins were invented only in the 7th century BC, payment was made in corn. This was measured using standard weights that were often carved in the shape of animals or birds, especially ducks.

"Lost-wax" metal casting
In about 3000 BC the "lost-wax" method of casting metal was invented, replacing the earlier technique of hammering. A model was made of wax, which was then covered with clay. When heated, the wax melted and was drained out. Hot liquid metal was then poured into the clay mold. When the metal became solid, the clay mold was broken open and the object was taken out. This method was used for a wide variety of objects, from arrowheads to life-size sculptures.

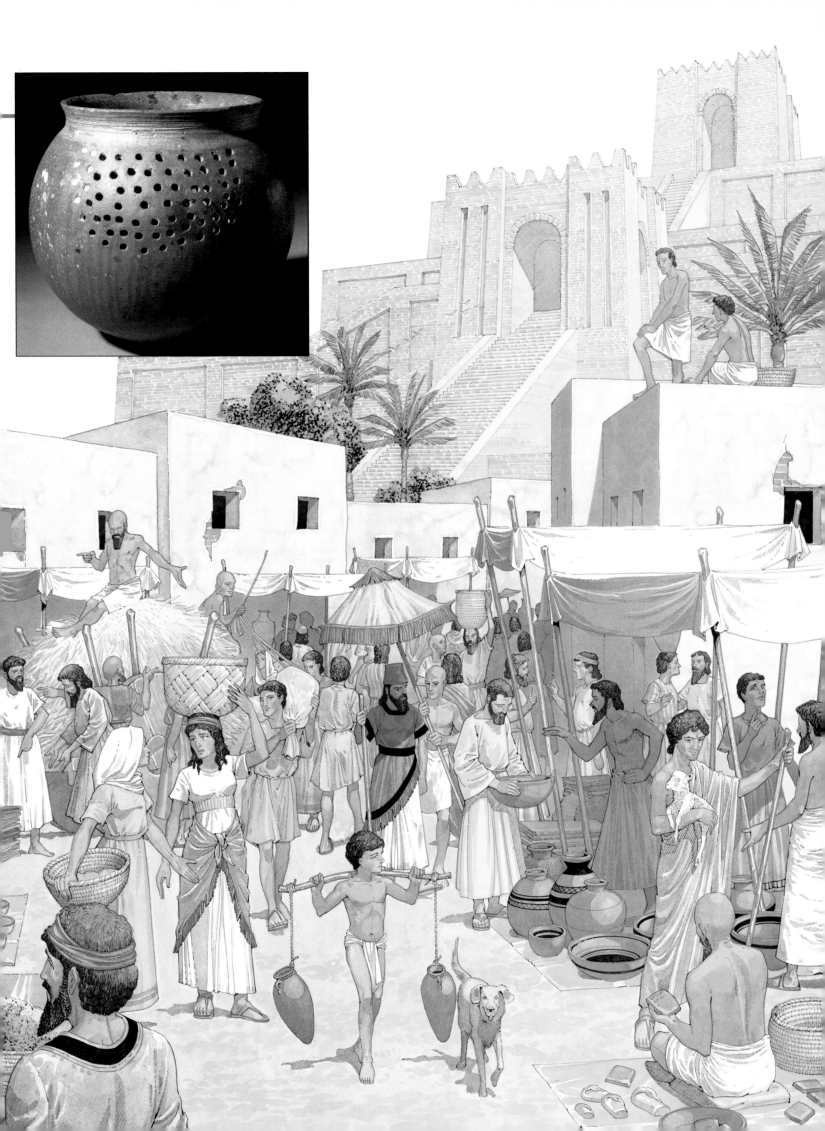

CHANGING KINGDOMS (1200–900 BC)

In about 1200 BC small groups of raiders emerged in the Near East and the Levant. The great Hittite empire crumbled, and Egypt was severely shaken. New political forces arose to shape the history of the Near East for the next 1,000 years and more.

The Sea Peoples

Egypt and the Levant were attacked by sea-faring raiders known as the "Sea Peoples." Pharaoh Ramesses III (1194–1163 BC) fought these invaders, who were probably made up of several different tribal groups. The Sea Peoples may have come from the Aegean in the west.

One of the seafaring tribes, driven out of Egypt by Ramesses III, settled on the Mediterranean coastal plains. These people were called the Philistines in the Bible, and their name lives on in the word Palestine. The Philistines adopted much of the local Canaanite culture, but their distinctive decorated pottery shows contact with Mycenaean (Greek) cultures.

Babylon and Assyria

Babylon remained under the rule of local kings. Its power grew again briefly under Nebucha-drezzar I (1126–1105 BC). He plundered the neighboring capital Susa, bringing back to Babylon the statue of Marduk that had been looted by the Elamite king Shutruk-Nahhunte in 1159 BC.

Assyria became a great power when Tiglath-Pileser I (1115–1077 BC) expanded its territories as far as the Levant. His campaigns against such peoples as the Ahlamu, or Aramaeans, were recorded in graphic detail on stone carvings at his palace in Nineveh, showing shocking war scenes. Tiglath-Pileser I also hunted wild elephants in northern Syria.

The Aramaeans

The Aramaeans were originally nomads who came from the Syrian desert. They established several small kingdoms in northern Syria and the Levant, blocking Assyria's advance to the Mediterranean. Aramaean power grew, and Adad-apla-iddina (1069–1048 BC), king of Babylon, was called the "Aramaean usurper." The Aramaeans spoke Aramaic, which replaced Akkadian as the main language of the Near East until Arabic emerged in 700 AD.

△ The triumph of the Egyptian pharaoh over his enemies is symbolized in this ivory carving. It shows a lion killing a Nubian (from northeast Africa), against a background of lilies and papyrus flowers.

▽ The infantry troops of Tiglath-Pileser I (1115–1077 BC) are laying siege to a city in Syria. Its gates are firmly shut, but its walls are being breached by a movable wooden siege-engine that is manned

from the inside and carries archers on top. The city's defending soldiers have leather-and-wicker shields. Their weapons are made from bronze, although iron was sometimes used at this time.

◁ A decorated pot from Ugarit, Syria. It dates from the 13th century BC. Similar vessels have been found in Cyprus.

◁ Female clay figurines, dating from about 900 BC, found near the coast of the Levant inhabited by the Philistines. They represent the goddess Astarte and emphasize fertility.

△ Modern Gaza on the coast of Israel. In the 12th and 11th centuries BC, it was the center of Philistine power and a gateway to Egypt along the coast. In the Bible, it is where Samson met his death.

Kings of Egypt, Assyria and Babylonia

Egypt
1194–1163 BC   Pharaoh Ramesses III

Assyria
1115–1066 BC   Tiglath-Pileser I

Babylonia (Second Dynasty of Isin)
1126–1105 BC   Nebuchadrezzar I
1069–1048 BC   Adad-apla-iddina

Elam
c.1159 BC   Shutruk-Nahhunte

▷ The Assyrian empire of Tiglath-Pileser I. The empire extended to the western Euphrates and was not troubled by the Sea Peoples who overran Egypt, the Levant, and Anatolia.

Scale 1 : 7 000 000

Assyria c.1500 BC
Extent of provincial control, 13th and 14th centuries BC
Area of direct provincial control under Tiglath-Pileser I (1115–1077 BC)
■ Known location of provincial capital

ISRAEL AND JUDAH

Pharaoh Merneptah's victory stele boasted in 1229 BC that "Israel is laid waste." He was not referring to a country but to another people who had recently emerged in the Near East.

The Bible and Israelite history

How the Israelites settled in the land of Canaan is recorded in the Bible. The book of Exodus describes their departure from Egypt and the wanderings of the 12 tribes in the Sinai peninsula region. The books of Joshua and Judges tell how the Israelites tried to settle in Canaan. They met with stiff resistance from the local inhabitants and the Philistines who lived on the rich coastal plain.

In about 1080 BC the Philistines tried to expand their control over the hill country where the Israelite tribes had settled. Faced by this threat, the loosely knit tribes united under the leadership of Saul, the first king of Israel. The two books of Samuel report the development of the Israelite monarchy.

King David

David was a brilliant king. He was installed as a vassal at Hebron in Judah by the Philistines. In 995 BC David threw off the Philistine overlordship and captured Jerusalem, the capital of the Jebusites, a Canaanite tribe.

David made Jerusalem his royal city. It was well placed to control his kingdom, which united Judah in the south with Israel in the north. David also made Jerusalem the religious center of the Israelite nation, bringing there the Ark of the Covenant (the sacred container of the scrolls of Jewish law) that the Philistines had captured earlier.

The Kingdom of Israel and Judah

David, 1000–962 BC
Reigns 7 years at Hebron, 33 years at Jerusalem, but these periods partly overlap

995 BC   David establishes capital at Jerusalem

Solomon, 962–922 (?) BC
The date given for Solomon's death varies from 935 to 928 to 922 BC, depending on the system of calculation used

▽ The united kingdom of Israel and Judah. Jerusalem, the capital city, was created by King David and made splendid by his son, King Solomon. When Solomon died the kingdom divided into Israel in the north and Judah in the south. In 924 BC the Egyptian pharaoh Shoshenq invaded, but the two kingdoms survived intact until the late 8th century BC.

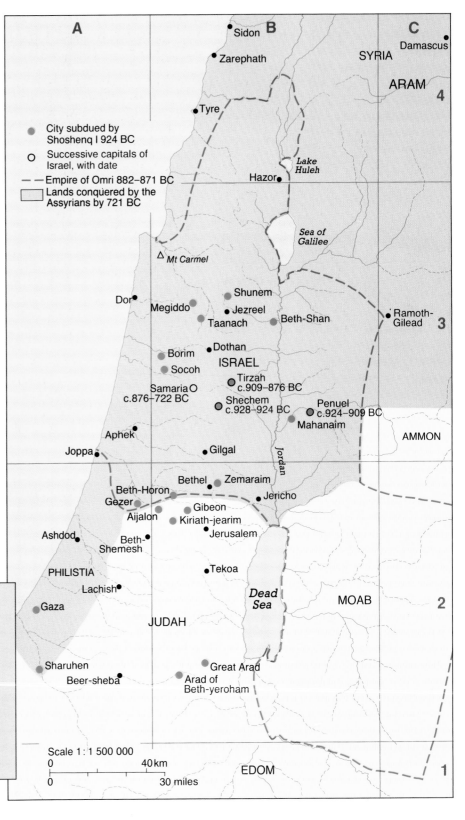

City subdued by Shoshenq I 924 BC
○ Successive capitals of Israel, with date
– – – Empire of Omri 882–871 BC
Lands conquered by the Assyrians by 721 BC

Solomon's achievements

King Solomon, David's son, built the Temple in Jerusalem to house the sacred Ark of the Covenant. The Muslim Dome of the Rock now occupies the same site. No trace of Solomon's building has been found, but descriptions are given in the Bible: 1 Kings, chs 5–8, and 2 Chronicles, chs 2–7. (Herod's temple was built centuries later.)

Solomon also built a palace, using luxury materials, such as ivory and beams of cedar and cypress wood. The design of his palace and the Temple was influenced by styles from Phoenicia, the cosmopolitan northern neighbor of the united kingdom of Israel and Judah.

Outside Jerusalem, there is more archaeological evidence of Solomon's building activities. Triple-chambered city gates that he had erected have been found at Megiddo, Hazor, and Gezer. At Megiddo there were also stables for hundreds of horses. Solomon's large army used horse-drawn chariots. At Ezion-Gezer on the Gulf of Aqaba, Solomon had an industrial complex for smelting copper.

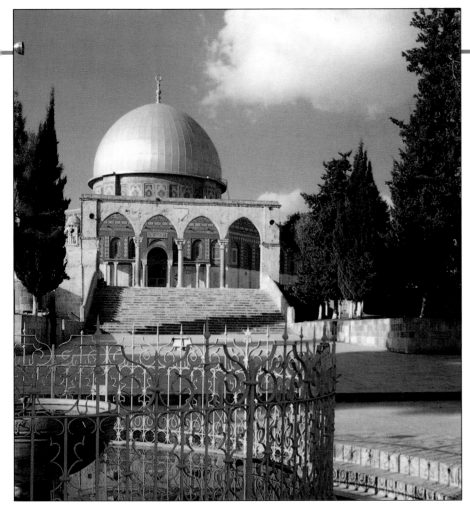

△ The Dome of the Rock is built over the rock where, according to tradition, Abraham was about to sacrifice Isaac, his only son. The beautiful shrine was completed in AD 691 and in medieval times was thought to be the center of the world.

▷ Solomon's Temple in Jerusalem. The plan of the building resembled Phoenician architecture. It was rectangular, with a porch flanked by a pair of bronze columns called Jachin and Boaz. The Holy Place was paneled in cedar wood with cypress-wood floors. Only the high priest could enter the Holy of Holies through its double doors. In the temple forecourt a huge bronze basin with water stood supported by 12 bronze bulls. This basin was used for rituals.

Kalhu

The city of Kalhu is in northern Iraq, at the ioin of the Tigris and Great Zab rivers, south of Mosul. The site is also called Nimrud. Kalhu became important when the Assyrian king Ashurnasirpal II (883–859 BC) selected it as his capital city. Shalmaneser III (858–824 BC) also built a palace there. Kalhu is mentioned in Genesis, ch. 10, as Calah.

Ashurnasirpal's city
By 878 BC, after Ashurnasirpal II had decided to move his capital from Ashur, a major building program began at Kalhu. A canal was dug from the Great Zab river to provide water. The city was enclosed in massive walls 5mi long that took 70 million bricks to build. Kalhu occupied 900 acres and included a ziggurat, temples, and a magnificent palace.

Ashurnasirpal was very proud of his new capital. An inscription at Kalhu describes a great feast that celebrated the completion of the Northwest Palace. The feasting lasted 10 days, and there were 69,574 guests from all parts of the Assyrian empire.

▽ The Northwest Palace at Kalhu. Around the outer courtyard were offices. The throne room was used for official functions. The king's private quarters were around the inner courtyard.

△ One of the ivory chairbacks that was found in a storage room at Fort Shalmaneser. It was probably made in northern Syria. The Assyrian kings' furniture was often decorated with ivory.

▽ How the throne room in the Northwest Palace might have looked – an artist's impression. Colored murals were set above the stone panels, and human-headed lions guarded the entrance.

outer courtyard

throne room

inner courtyard

tombs of queens

contours at 6.6ft intervals

0   20   40 m
0   50   100   150 ft

Kalhu's sculptures

Carved stone panels decorated the courtyard walls and the adjoining throne room of the Northwest Palace. They recorded the king at war and hunting, and fulfilling his religious duties. Ashurnasirpal is also shown receiving gifts, including monkeys, from foreigners. The reliefs, which were once brightly painted, also record in fine detail the fabrics, clothes, and jewelry of the king and his officials.

Treasures of Kalhu

Three royal tombs were excavated at Kalhu, and their treasures were found intact. Gold jewelry was discovered in mint condition.

Thousands of fragments of carved ivory were discovered at an arsenal called Fort Shalmaneser and in a well. Many pieces had been war booty collected by the Assyrians during their campaigns in the Levant. They had been hidden there for safe keeping when the Medes sacked Kalhu in 612 BC.

▷ One of the treasures found in the royal tombs at Kalhu. This gold wristlet was set with a precious agate-stone and inlaid with enamel. Gold winged genies hold buckets and pinecones. The wall reliefs at Kalhu show the kings wearing similar wristlets.

THE LATE ASSYRIAN EMPIRE (1000–750 BC)

After being weakened for several centuries by the raids of the Aramaeans, the Assyrians grew powerful again in about 900 BC. Adad-nirari II (911–891 BC) defeated Babylonia and seized control of the Khabur region in the east. His son Tukulti-Ninurta II (890–884 BC) and his grandson Ashurnasirpal II (883–859 BC) continued his military successes.

Ashurnasirpal II went to war every year. Although his claim to be always victorious was probably untrue, in 877 BC he reached the Mediterranean. He called it "the Great Sea of the land Amurru."

Ashurnasirpal received much tribute from the rich Phoenician states, including "gold, silver, tin, bronze, a bronze cauldron, linen garments with multicolored trimmings, a large female ape and a small female ape, ebony, boxwood, ivory, and sea creatures." He probably used many of these items in the construction of his splendid palace at Kalhu.

▽ The Balawat gates, a pair of massive bronze-clad gates built by Shalmaneser III and found 10mi northeast of Kalhu. The detail here (*left*) shows chariots with six-spoked wheels, as was the custom in the 9th century, on campaign in Babylonia. Each "leaf" of the gates was about 6.5ft wide and 13ft high. Sixteen embossed bands of bronze were engraved with scenes from Shalmaneser's conquests, including campaigns against the Urartu, who lived in the Lake Van region of present-day Turkey.

Shalmaneser III and Ahab of Israel

Shalmaneser III (858–824 BC) brought Assyrian power to a new height. After conquering the Aramaean state of Bit Adini in 854 BC, the next year he led his armies against an alliance of kings that included Ben-Hadad of Damascus and Ahab of Israel (869–850 BC). Ahab had 10,000 foot soldiers and 2,000 chariots.

Shalmaneser was the first Assyrian ruler to come into contact with an Israelite king. After the battle, at Qarqar on the Orontes river, he erected the Black Obelisk (a tall stone monument) at Kalhu and inscribed on it his claims of an overwhelming victory. The biblical account in 1 Kings, ch. 20, suggests that Shalmaneser's success was more limited, but by 838 BC most states in the region had to pay him tribute.

Shamsi-Adad V (823–811 BC) on a stele from Kalhu. The king is in his court robes and is wearing the Assyrian royal headdress and diadem.

▽ Detail from the Black Obelisk of Shalmaneser III (858–824 BC). The cuneiform inscription identifies the man on his knees kissing the ground before the king as the Israelite king Jehu. The camels were tribute from Egypt.

Friendship with Babylon, then war

In 851 BC Shalmaneser III helped the king of Babylon defeat a revolt against him. The two kings regarded each other as equals and allies. A throne-base found at Kalhu shows both men clasping hands. Shalmaneser III respected Babylonian religion and visited the temples of Marduk at Babylon and Nabu at Borsippa. He also gave the local citizens gifts and banquets. This was unusual, because the Assyrian king usually demanded vast amounts of tribute.

By the time of Shamshi-Adad V (823–811 BC), the alliance with Babylon was over, and war broke out between the two kingdoms.

ASSYRIA TRIUMPHANT (750–626 BC)

Strong kings took the Assyrian empire to the peak of its power between 750 BC and 626 BC. They are mentioned in the Bible (2 Kings).

Tiglath-Pileser III and Shalmaneser V

Tiglath-Pileser III (744–727 BC) was a successful ruler. He reorganized the army and replaced vassal kings with loyal provincial governors. He introduced a "royal mail" service – his messengers traveled in chariots drawn by mules to all parts of the empire. Tiglath-Pileser III also deported many of the people he conquered to curb future rebellions.

Shalmaneser V (726–722 BC) succeeded his father. Records of his short reign have not survived, but the Bible (2 Kings, ch. 17, verses 3–6) tells how he captured Israel when King Hosea rebelled. Shalmaneser V may have died in the three-year siege of Samaria.

▽ The Assyrian empire in the late 8th century BC. The capital city of the empire was Ashur in northern Mesopotamia. The lands controlled by the Assyrians extended from Ur near The Gulf and included the kingdom of Israel. Jerusalem and the kingdom of Judah only came under their control between 733 BC and 650 BC. An efficient road system linked the distant parts of the empire, with travelers' rest-houses at regular intervals along the highways.

Sargon

How Sargon (722–705 BC) came to be king is unknown, but he was a capable leader. At Qarqar, on the Orontes river, Sargon defeated an alliance of Syrian states, establishing Assyrian control as far as Egypt. In Asia Minor he controlled the Phrygians, whose king was the legendary Midas. In 714 BC he destroyed Musasir, capital of the Urartu. The kings of Cyprus paid tribute to him. In 709 BC Sargon became king of Babylon, ruling the Near East from The Gulf to the Sinai desert. Sargon was killed in a minor clash in 705 BC.

Kings of Assyria 744–626 BC	
744–727 BC	Tiglath-Pileser III
726–722 BC	Shalmaneser V
721–705 BC	Sargon II
704–681 BC	Sennacherib
680–669 BC	Esarhaddon
668–626 BC	Ashurbanipal

Scale 1 : 8 000 000

0 — 200 km

0 — 150 miles

Assyrian empire
- At the beginning of Tiglath-Pileser III's reign
- Maximum extent under Sargon II
- ▲ Location of stele or rock relief
- Amid Correspondent with Sargon
- — Principal route

Sargon's successors

Sennacherib (704–681 BC) was Sargon's son. His capture of Lachish in 701 BC and his dealings with Hezekiah, king of Judah, are recorded in the Bible (2 Kings, ch. 18). Problems with Babylon occupied Sennacherib until 694 BC, when he destroyed the city. One of his own sons then murdered him.

Esarhaddon (680–669 BC), Sargon's crown prince, then claimed the throne. He captured Memphis from the Egyptians in 671 BC, but died on a second campaign in 669 BC.

Esarhaddon's two crown princes succeeded him. Ashurbanipal, king of Assyria, overshadowed his brother, the king of Babylon, both as a military leader and as a man of learning. Ashurbanipal collected many cuneiform texts for his library at Nineveh.

◁ A stone carving recording one of the campaigns of the Assyrian kings. Here an Assyrian soldier is shown cutting off the head of the Elamite king whom Ashurbanipal defeated in 635 BC.

▽ A royal procession enters Babylon through the Ishtar gate. It was over 46ft high and made of brilliant blue-glazed bricks decorated with bulls and dragons, symbols of the gods. The king rides in his horse-drawn chariot, sheltered by an umbrella, the symbol of royalty. The first chariot carries his senior court official.

Ashur

Ashur lies on a rocky outcrop of land overlooking the Tigris river in northern Iraq. It had been an outpost of southern influence from about 2300 BC. Sumerian-style statues from the Early Dynastic period and inscriptions were found here.

City of trade

Ashur was situated on an important trade route to Anatolia, where in about 2000 BC merchants from the city established a trading colony at Kanesh. Donkey caravans carried woolen textiles and tin that had been mined in Iran to Ashur, from where they were distributed farther afield. Many cuneiform tablets discovered at Kanesh show that a lively correspondence went on between the two depots.

Assyrian capital

Although Ashur was well placed for trade, it was not an obvious site for the capital of a kingdom, because of the lack of farmland around it. Despite this, the Middle and Late Assyrian rulers favored the city.

Adad-nirari I (1305–1274 BC) built a large palace at Ashur. Tukulti-Ninurta I (1243–1207 BC) dug a moat around the western side of the city, which was open to attack. He also rebuilt the Ishtar temple and started work on a new palace.

Ashur kept its reputation as a religious center even after Ashurnasirpal II (883–859 BC) shifted his capital to Kalhu. There was a ziggurat and many temples, apart from the major shrine to Ashur, the city god who was a combination of the Sumerian god Enlil and the Babylonian deity Marduk. The tombs of five Assyrian kings have been found at Ashur. These include those of Ashurnasirpal II and Shamsi-Adad V (823–811 BC).

Between 614 BC and 612 BC the Medes from Iran invaded Assyria and looted Ashur. In the 1st and 2nd centuries it was resettled and became known as Labbana. Now the site is threatened by flooding from a proposed dam farther upstream on the Tigris.

△ The tomb and sarcophagus (stone coffin) of the Middle Assyrian king Ashur-belkals (1074–1057 BC), one of five royal burial places discovered at Ashur.

▽ The site of Ashur. There were many temples, including the temple of the city god, also called Ashur. The palace, the ziggurat and the temples were sited on the steep northern cliffs overlooking the old course of the Tigris. The river now flows on the eastern side of the promontory. The western side was protected by a wall and a moat.

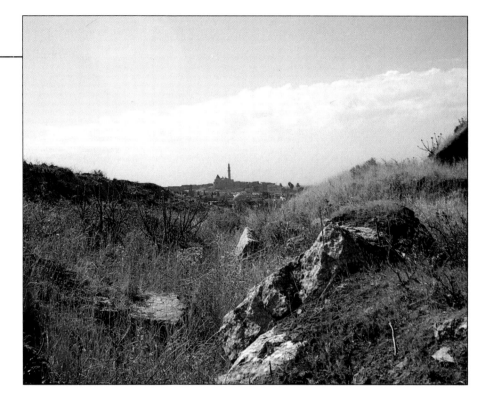

Nineveh

Nineveh was one of the greatest cities of Mesopotamia. It is situated on the eastern side of the Tigris river near modern Mosul in northern Iraq. The site was enclosed by more than 7½mi of city walls and has two main mounds: Nebi Yunus and Kuyunjik.

Under the dynasty of Agade, Manishtushu (2269–2255 BC) founded the famous temple of Ishtar at Nineveh, mentioned by Hammurabi in his law code. Here was found the superb bronze life-sized head of Naram-Sin (2254–2218 BC), one of the great Mesopotamian art treasures.

The Late Assyrian ruler Sennacherib (705–681 BC) made Nineveh his capital. His Southwest Palace was decorated with carved stone reliefs showing, among other scenes, the siege and capture of Lachish. Sennacherib's grandson Ashurbanipal (669–627 BC) built the North Palace on Kuyunjik, for his cuneiform library.

Genesis, ch. 10, verse 11, mentions Nineveh, and the biblical books of Nahum and Jonah prophesy the city's downfall. In 612 BC Nineveh was destroyed by the Babylonians and Medes. Its fall marked the collapse of the Assyrian empire.

△ A view across Nineveh, from the mound of Kuyunjik to Nebi Yunus, the traditional Muslim burial site of the prophet Jonah. The tall minaret of the mosque now marks the location of the grave.

▽ Ashurbanipal and his queen Ashur-sharrat feast in their gardens – possibly those of the Northwest Palace at Nineveh, where the carving was found. In the pine tree on the left hangs the head of an enemy king.

WARFARE

The first weapons were the stone and wooden tools used to hunt animals: arrowheads, clubs, spears, and slings. Then came metal weapons. Copper axes, spears, and daggers were in use by about 4000 BC. There were bronze weapons by about 2000 BC, and iron 1,000 years later.

How early wars were fought

Armies were well organized. The Sumerian "Stele of the Vultures," dated 2450 BC, shows soldiers from Lagash. The men march in military formation with their spears and axes, protected by their shields, behind their leader, Eannatum. In Sumer, the warrior-*lugals* or "great men" became the first kings.

The first fortified city was Jericho, whose massive walls were built as long ago as 9000 BC. As more cities constructed similar defenses, siege warfare developed as a way of capturing these places. Military machinery, such as battering rams and siege towers, came into use by about 1000 BC.

Horses revolutionized war. Slow-moving carts drawn by mules had been used in Sumerian times. In about 1500 BC the first two-wheeled horse-drawn war-chariots were used. Cavalry units, introduced by the Assyrians, rode bareback, because the saddle had not yet been invented.

◁ The "Stele of the Vultures" is the first known carving showing an army at war. On the lower part of this fragment, King Eannatum rides in a chariot, followed by his foot soldiers. This may be a victory parade to celebrate the success of the war shown in the upper part of the fragment.

△ Flints (*left*) were still used for arrowheads after metal weapons were cast. Personal weapons, such as these daggers (*middle*), were often beautifully decorated. Maces (*right*) were both weapons and symbols of royal authority – just the heads are shown here.

◁ Assyrian cavalrymen from the reliefs at the Northwest Palace at Kalhu. The men ride in pairs, one steering the horses, and the other shooting with bow and arrow. Their defeated enemies lie trampled and decapitated under the horses' hooves.

▷ A crescent-shaped bronze axhead dating from about 2400 BC. The axhead was fitted into a slot in the haft (wooden handle) and fastened with nails or bolts. Other axheads were cast in metal with a hole to take the haft.

The Assyrian army and its commanders

The Assyrian army was a well-developed fighting machine, with as many as 50,000 troops. It received its supplies through taxes, tribute, and war booty. Some of the soldiers were mercenaries – foreign professional soldiers who fought for money.

The king was always the commander-in-chief of the army. Provincial governors often acted as the generals. Sometimes senior palace officials also led the troops. Tiglath-Pileser III (744–727 BC) appointed his chief eunuch commander of his chariot forces. Before going into battle, kings would consult omen-tellers who would reveal the will of the gods.

The infantry

The infantry or foot soldiers were a large and important part of the Assyrian army. The men came from the poorer families or were slaves sent by their wealthy owners.

The light infantry uniform was a short tunic, a cone-shaped helmet and a lightweight shield made of wicker and leather. The heavy infantry uniform was a long robe covered with metal plates. This was one of the earliest forms of chain mail and made a weighty load. The weapons of the infantryman included a sling (for throwing stones), a longbow, and a pike.

It was the job of the infantry to force its way through holes broken in the walls of cities being besieged. Archers were positioned in the top of assault towers which were made of wicker and leather on a wooden frame. The towers were wheeled and had battering rams.

Chariot warfare

Fewer in number than the infantry, the chariot troops of the Assyrian army were usually high-born Assyrians. They were the army's élite. Chariots were manned by a charioteer and an archer, sometimes protected by two shield-bearers. Chariots were drawn by two horses, sometimes with a third horse not yoked to the chariot but kept as a spare to replace an exhausted beast in battle.

The body of the chariots was square and probably made of wickerwork, with the wheel axle at the back end. Chariots were open at the back. Spears, the battle ax, and other weapons were kept in a box attached to the front.

▽ The art of war in Assyrian times. The bronze panels of the Balawat gates show scenes from the wars fought by the Assyrians. Here an Assyrian siege engine, with archers on top, attacks a city in northern Syria. Siege warfare was an important part of the Assyrians' method of conquest and is depicted in their reliefs.

▽ This detail from the Balawat gates shows Phoenician boats bringing tribute from the island of Tyre to the mainland for Shalmaneser III. Both the Assyrians and, later, the Persians used the famous Phoenician navy in warfare.

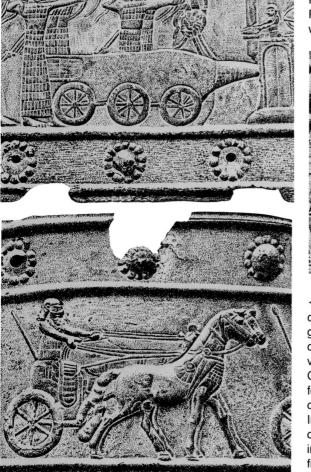

◁ An Assyrian war-chariot, from the Balawat gates. Shalmaneser III's chariot forces were the very best part of his army. Chariots were also used for hunting and in ceremonial processions. In the late 8th century BC cavalry became more important, especially for fighting in the mountains, where chariots could not go.

BABYLONIAN REVIVAL (626–560 BC)

The Late Assyrian period was a troubled time for Babylon, which had 24 kings between 900 BC and 681 BC. The city's fortunes changed when Esarhaddon (680–669 BC) became king. By the end of the next century Babylon became rich, powerful, and famous.

Nabopolassar

Nabopolassar (625–605 BC), who claimed to be the "son of a nobody," founded the New Babylonian dynasty. After 10 years of fighting the Assyrians in the Babylonian territories, Nabopolassar gained enough power to march north. He intended to attack Ashur, the religious capital of the Assyrians.

Before Nabopolassar could strike, Ashur was overrun by the Medes, from northwest Iran. The Babylonian and Median armies joined forces and in 612 BC captured Nineveh, looting the palaces and temples.

In 1990 a tangled mass of skeletons was excavated at one of the city's gates – evidence of Nineveh's population trying to flee. Assyria's power had ended.

Neo-Babylonian kings
The Chaldean dynasty, 625–562 BC

625–605 BC   Nabopolassar
614 BC   Destruction of Ashur
612 BC   Sack of Nineveh

605–562 BC   Nebuchadrezzar
605 BC   Defeat of Pharaoh Necho at Carchemish, in Syria

Kings of Judah, 640–587 BC

640–609 BC   Josiah
Josiah takes advantage of Assyria's weakness to re-establish the Davidic kingdom but is killed in 609 BC by Pharaoh Necho II at Megiddo

609–598 BC   Jehoiakim

598–597 BC   Jehoiachin
597 BC   Jehoiachin deported to Babylon

597–587 BC   Zedekiah
587 BC   Siege of Jerusalem, destruction of the Temple, deportation of citizens to Babylon

▽ Nebuchadrezzar and his wife relax in the beautiful Hanging Gardens of Babylon. They are being fanned by servants and entertained by a court musician playing a harp. The king and queen wear embroidered garments decorated with sequins made of gold. They are enjoying drinks chilled with ice from the royal icehouse. An icehouse was found at the palace of Zimri-Lim at Mari dating from about 2000 BC.

△ A bull from the foundations of the Ishtar Gate at Babylon. Like other bulls and dragons featured on the underground foundations, it was made from molded baked bricks. Above ground the upper part of the gate was decorated with similar figures.

The bulls were the symbol of Adad, god of thunder. The dragons had horns and were the symbols of Marduk, the city god of Babylon. The great processions that took place during the 11-day Akitu or New Year festival would have passed through these gates.

Nebuchadrezzar

Before he became king, Nebuchadrezzar, Nabopolassar's son and crown-prince, had tasted success in battle. In 605 BC he defeated the Egyptian pharaoh Necho at Carchemish in northern Syria. He left the kingdom of Judah alone, because King Jehoiakim had paid him tribute. On the death of his father in 605 BC, Nebuchadrezzar returned to Babylon to be crowned king. He had marched for three weeks, covering over 30mi a day, to return for his coronation.

Babylon and the Jews

Jehoiakim (609–598 BC) succeeded his father Josiah (640–609 BC) as king of Judah. He accepted Nebuchadrezzar as his overlord. Then, in 601–600 BC, Jehoiakim rebelled. Nebuchadrezzar captured Jerusalem in 597 BC. He took Judah's new king, Jehoiachin, the son of Jehoiakim, and his mother, wives, and officials in chains to Babylon.

Nebuchadrezzar appointed Jehoiachin's uncle, Zedekiah (597–587 BC), king of Judah. But Zedekiah also rebelled. The Babylonians laid siege to Jerusalem, and broke through its defenses in 587–586 BC. They destroyed much of the city, deporting the Jewish population and carrying away treasures from the Temple. The Bible records these events in the books of 2 Kings, 2 Chronicles and Jeremiah.

Nebuchadrezzar's great city

Nebuchadrezzar restored Babylon's wealth and reputation. He took a leading role in the great Akitu festival, marking the Babylonian New Year. He carried out massive rebuilding programs at the temple of Marduk and the ziggurat, as well as constructing the fabled Hanging Gardens for one of his wives, who was homesick for the mountains of her native Media. Nebuchadrezzar also surrounded Babylon with walls that encircled an area of more than 3sq mi.

△ This black stone tablet has an inscription recording the rebuilding of Babylon and its temples by Esarhaddon (the city's king from 680 BC to 669 BC). It shows the Assyrian king holding his mace, the symbol of royal power, and standing respectfully before a temple. Just behind him is the sacred tree of life and the bull, symbol of the weather god. The plow below suggests the agricultural and economic wealth that Esarhaddon restored to Babylon.

Babylon

"Babylon surpasses in splendor any city of the known world", wrote the Greek historian Herodotus, who visited Babylon in about 450 BC. The site is about 50mi south of Baghdad, in present-day Iraq. The city became important under Hammurabi (1792–1750 BC). But it resisted Assyrian rule and was destroyed by Sennacherib (705–681 BC).

In the Neo-Babylonian period, Babylon was capital of the empire. Nebopolassar and his son Nebuchadrezzar (605–562 BC) carried out a huge building program. The city remained important under the later Persian rulers, opening its gates to Cyrus in 539 BC. Alexander the Great also entered the city without resistance. When Alexander's general Seleucus built his new capital farther along the Tigris river, Babylon sank into decline.

"Gates of the gods"

The name Babylon means "gate of the gods." The site was roughly rectangular and had a double wall of defense. Entry to the city was through eight gateways, each protected by a god or goddess. The most spectacular was the gate dedicated to Ishtar, with its brilliant blue tiles decorated with bulls and dragons.

The Hanging Gardens

Ancient historians rated the Hanging Gardens of Babylon as one of the seven wonders of the world. But no mention of them has been found in Babylonian writings of the period, and no site for them has been located. A vaulted building on which the gardens were supposed to have grown was probably a palace storehouse which may have been cooled by vegetation on its roof.

▽ Ancient Babylon covered an area of over 2,150 acres – larger than many modern towns. At the time of Nebuchadrezzar, the Euphrates river flowed through the city, dividing it into two sections, which were connected by a bridge. In the older, eastern part (*left*) was the king's palace, near the Ishtar gate (*bottom left*). From here the processional way led toward the great temple of Marduk and the ziggurat (*top center*). The western part of Babylon (*right*) was probably a residential area.

Babylon

◁ A glazed relief brick panel from Darius' palace at Susa. The winged lion has ram's horns and is decorated in blues and greens. Embossed colored tiles developed because of the lack of stone in the region.

△ Basalt statue of the lion of Babylon trampling a man beneath him. This was found in the ruins of the Northern Palace, which was built by Nebuchadrezzar. It was part of a "museum" belonging to the king.

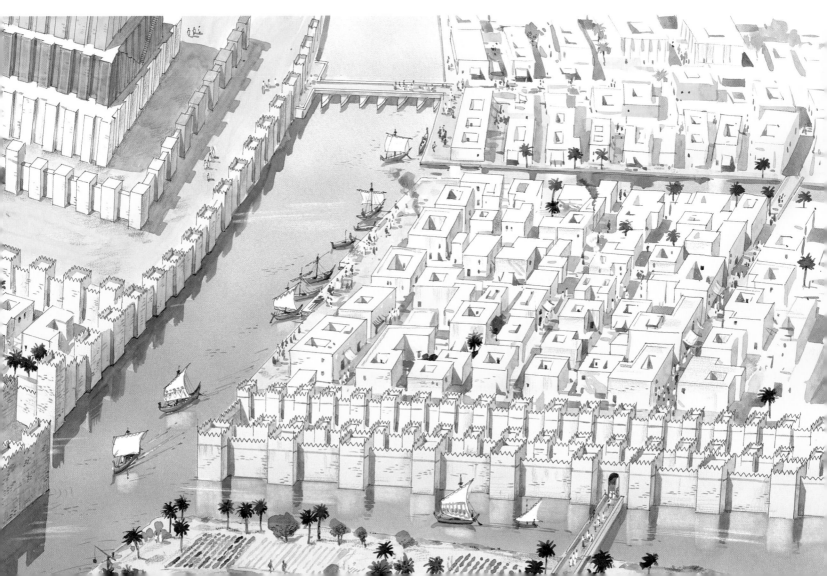

RISE OF THE PERSIAN EMPIRE (560–521 BC)

Cyrus became king of the Persians in 559 BC. The Median king Astyges was his overlord. Other rulers of the time were Croesus of Lydia and Nabonidus of Babylon. Cyrus conquered all three kings and founded the Persian empire, which dominated the Near East for the next 200 years.

The conquests of Cyrus (559–530 BC)

In 550 BC Cyrus turned against Astyges, king of the Medes. The Medes had overrun the cities of Ashur, Kalhu, and Nineveh in 612–614 BC, ending the Assyrian dynasty. Now Cyrus marched to the Median capital at Hamadan, emptied the treasury and took possession of vast lands from Turkey to Central Asia.

In 547 BC Cyrus led his armies to the western borders of his empire to do battle with the Lydians. Croesus, the Lydian king, was legendary for his wealth. There was gold in his lands, and the Lydians may have been the first people to use large numbers of coins, stamped to guarantee their quality and weight.

Croesus' territories included the Greek cities of the Aegean coast. When Croesus heard of Cyrus' defeat of the Medes, he thought he could expand his empire. He consulted the oracle at Delphi before going to war and learned that a great empire would be destroyed. Croesus did not realize that the empire to be destroyed was his – at the hands of Cyrus.

Babylon: jewel in Cyrus' crown

The Babylonian king Nabonidus (555–539 BC) was more than 60 years old when he came to the throne. He rebuilt the temple to Sin in Harran and installed his daughter as the priestess of Sin at Ur. This was a time of poverty, plague, and famine in Babylon. For unknown reasons, Nabonidus left Babylon to live in Taima, in northwest Arabia. He left his son Belshazzar to rule in his place, and for 10 years the Akitu or New Year's festival could not be celebrated, because there was no king.

Nabonidus was unpopular with the people of Babylon for neglecting the religion of the city's god, Marduk. In 539 BC the Akitu festival was celebrated, as is described by the Greek historians and the biblical book of Daniel. The end of the Babylonian dynasty had arrived.

▽ The growth of the Persian empire. Cyrus' vast lands stretched from the coast of the Mediterranean to the Indus valley. The Persians had been ruled by the Medes when Cyrus became king. Within a few years he had conquered the territories of the Medes, which stretched to Central Asia in the east, the Babylonian lands in the south, and the Lydian kingdom, in modern Turkey, in the west. Cyrus' son Cambyses also controlled Egypt.

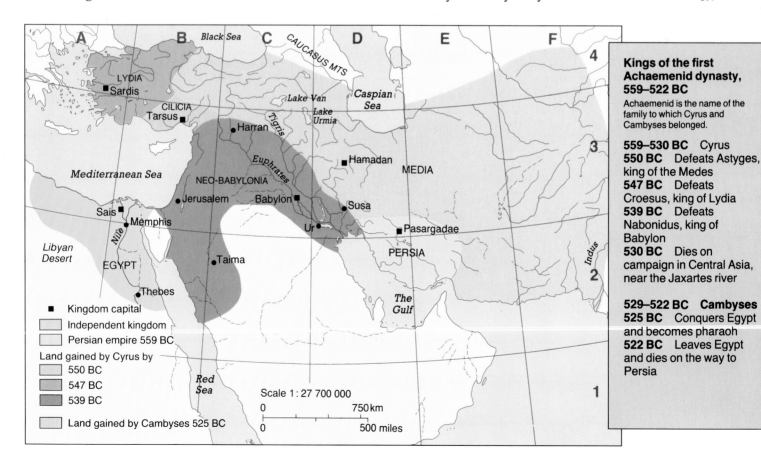

Kings of the first Achaemenid dynasty, 559–522 BC

Achaemenid is the name of the family to which Cyrus and Cambyses belonged.

559–530 BC Cyrus
550 BC Defeats Astyges, king of the Medes
547 BC Defeats Croesus, king of Lydia
539 BC Defeats Nabonidus, king of Babylon
530 BC Dies on campaign in Central Asia, near the Jaxartes river

529–522 BC Cambyses
525 BC Conquers Egypt and becomes pharaoh
522 BC Leaves Egypt and dies on the way to Persia

■ Kingdom capital
Independent kingdom
Persian empire 559 BC
Land gained by Cyrus by
550 BC
547 BC
539 BC
Land gained by Cambyses 525 BC

Scale 1 : 27 700 000
0 ... 750km
0 ... 500 miles

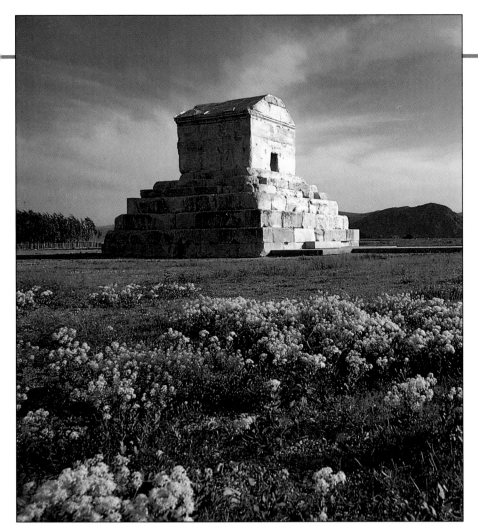

Cyrus arrived with his army at Babylon in 539 BC and entered the city without a battle. The Babylonians did not resist. Many of them, celebrating a religious festival, did not even know. Cyrus told his troops not to damage the city or its temples.

Foundation of the Persian empire

Cyrus proclaimed himself "king of the world, great king . . . king of Babylon, king of Sumer and Akkad." The Greek historians considered him a model ruler. He allowed the Jews who had been exiled in Babylon by Nebuchadrezzar to return to Jerusalem and rebuild the Temple, as the biblical book of Ezra relates.

Cyrus used Lydian craftsmen to build his capital at Pasargadae, in modern Iran. He was buried there in 530 BC after being killed in battle in Central Asia.

Cyrus' son, Cambyses (529–522 BC), expanded the empire to include Egypt, which he conquered in 525 BC. Cambyses had the reputation of being a tyrant. He lived in Egypt and acted like a pharaoh. In 522 BC he left Egypt to return to Persia but died on the way.

△ Cyrus had his own tomb built at Pasargadae, his capital. It is a simple gabled building set on a stepped platform. Cyrus' modesty is shown in an inscription that was on the tomb: "I am Cyrus, who founded the empire of the Persians and was king of Asia. Grudge me not therefore this monument".

▷ Remains of a palace at Pasargadae. The city's palaces were inspired by Median architecture and are not like those in Mesopotamia. They had columned halls and open porticoes which allowed access to the beautiful gardens in which they were set. Lydian stonemasons may have made the columns, which are similar to ones found at Ephesus in western Turkey.

THE EMPIRE OF DARIUS (521–486 BC)

Darius (521–486 BC) ruled the Persian empire after Cambyses. Under his brilliant rule, the empire reached into Europe, but he had come to the throne only after a struggle.

The Behistun inscription

Darius told the world about his fight to become king, after Cambyses died in 522 BC, in the famous inscription of Behistun. Carved on a rock overlooking the main caravan route from Babylon to Hamadan in northern Iran, the inscription is in three languages: Old Persian, Babylonian, and Elamite.

Darius claimed that after Cambyses murdered his own brother, Bardiya, before setting out to Egypt, a priest called Gaumata

▽ Building materials for the palace at Susa. Darius made the city of Susa the capital of his huge empire. He imported materials from every corner of his territories to build his palace there. In 500 BC he built a canal from the river Nile to the Red Sea, making it much easier to bring goods by ship from Egypt. Darius was proud of the resources used and left inscriptions at Susa listing the people and materials involved in building his palace.

seized the throne. He pretended to be Bardiya and was accepted as king. Nobody dared resist Gaumata until Darius killed him in 522 BC.

The real truth is probably that Darius took the Persian throne by force from Cambyses' brother. Darius did belong to the Achaemenid family, after which the dynasty is named, but was not in direct line to the throne.

Rebellions broke out in many parts of the Persian empire after Cambyses died. Within a year Darius had established his rule over the kings of Persia, Elam, Media, Assyria, Egypt, Parthia, Margian, Sattagydia, and Scythia. This achievement is recorded on the relief accompanying the Behistun inscription. The carving shows Darius under the winged standard of Ahura-Mazda, the great god of the Zoroastrian religion, receiving the homage of the nine kings.

Darius believed that he had been chosen to rule by the supreme god, Ahura-Mazda. He thought that kingship was a gift from the gods and that kings had special responsibilities to their people.

At Naqsh-i Rastam, where Darius was buried in a rock-cut tomb, an inscription proclaimed that Darius had been made king by Ahura-Mazda; he was a friend to good and an enemy to evil; he protected the weak from the strong and also the strong from the weak; he desired what was right; he was a good horseman, a good archer, and a good spearman.

The Persian empire under Darius

Darius' empire reached from Central Asia to Egypt. He conquered the Indus region and in 513 BC campaigned against the Scythians in Thrace, on the Black Sea. He went into Europe, crossing the river Danube.

In 499 BC the Greeks who lived in Cyprus and on the Aegean coast of Turkey rebelled against the Persians. The Ionian revolt lasted six years. Darius used the Phoenician navy to regain Cyprus, but the Greek cities on the Turkish coast were harder to control.

In 494 BC a naval battle took place off the island of Lade, near Miletus. The Persian fleet of 600 ships overwhelmed the much smaller Greek navy. Darius now turned his attention to mainland Greece, but the Greeks defeated the Persian army at Marathon in 490 BC.

Darius died in 486 BC. His son Xerxes inherited a very well-organized empire, with a regular taxation system and efficient communications. Like the Assyrians before them, the Persians relied on a quick horseback messenger service with relay stations providing fresh mounts.

▽ This molded and glazed brick panel from Susa was made in the 12th century BC but was thrown away by Darius. This form of ornamental brickwork was first produced by the Kassites in Mesopotamia then used by the Persians.

△ Darius was king over many nations. Delegations brought gifts to him, as shown in this stone carving. The Bactrian (from Bactria in Central Asia) holds a pair of bracelets similar to some found in Afghanistan today.

Susa

Susa is situated on the plains of Khuzestan in southwest Iran. In about 2500 BC the city was the capital of Elam, which had links with the Fars region and with Anshan to the southeast. With the rise of the dynasty of Agade in 2300 BC Susa came under Mesopotamian control. In 2004 BC it was reunited with Anshan, beginning the Elamite era. Almost 800 years later, in one of the most brilliant periods of their history, the Elamites overran Mesopotamia and brought its finest art treasures as war booty to Susa.

Ashurbanipal (668–627 BC) captured Susa and completely destroyed it. He sowed the fields with salt so that no crops could grow.

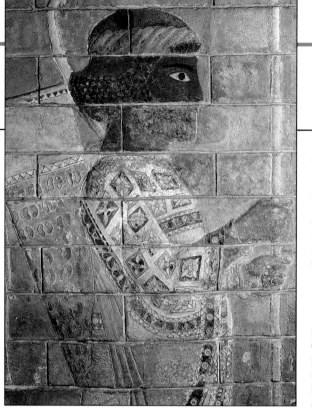

◁ A glazed brick relief from Darius' palace at Susa. The archer was probably a member of Darius' bodyguard. This decorated brickwork may have been made by Mesopotamian workers who were brought to Susa.

▽ The fronts of two bulls placed together made the column capitals (topmost parts) for the palace at Susa. A heavy wooden beam rested on the animals' backs.

◁ This gold statue of a man with a kid is one of a pair. The other is made from silver. Both statues were probably gifts of thanks made by a private person to the temple at Susa. They are not Persian but from an earlier period, about 1100 BC.

▽ The site of Susa, which was identified in 1851, has four mounds. Three of these – the palace, the acropolis or "high place," which was the main religious center, and the royal city – belong to the period of the Persian empire.

City of Darius

The time of the Persian empire was a golden period for Susa. The city blossomed under Darius the Great (522–486 BC), who made it his administrative capital. On the Apadana mound of the city he built a large palace, using workers and luxury materials from all parts of the Persian empire, and combining Babylonian and Median architecture.

Darius' palace at Susa is mentioned in the biblical books of Esther and Nehemiah, where the city is called Shushan.

Alexander the Great captured Susa in 331 BC. To cement his empire together, he arranged the mass marriage of Greek soldiers and Persian women there. The tomb of the biblical prophet Daniel is thought to be near the acropolis area, now the village of Shush, and is still visited by Muslim pilgrims.

THE END OF THE ANCIENT NEAR EAST (486–323 BC)

The last years of the Persian empire were a time of struggle with the Greeks. The Persians gained some early victories, but these were followed by defeats.

Xerxes (486–465 BC) against the Greeks

Darius' son Xerxes was his chosen successor. According to Herodotus, the Greek historian, Xerxes led 2 million men against Greece in 480 BC. He captured Athens, but the Greek navy defeated the Persian fleet at the battle of Salamis. Xerxes returned to Persia, leaving his general Mardonius in command. After an undecided land battle at Plataea in 479 BC, the Persian armies left Greece, but the Persian fleet was again defeated, this time at Mycale in Ionia.

Murder in the Persian court

Despite the Greek defeats, the Persian empire remained intact until Xerxes died, or was perhaps killed by three of his courtiers, in 465 BC. Now the Persian court entered a period of plots and multiple murders, often by poisoning. One of Xerxes' sons killed another. Then, in 425 BC, three of Xerxes' grandsons ruled in quick succession, the first two being murdered after only a few months on the throne. More royal conspiracies and murders followed for almost 100 years.

Darius III and Alexander

Darius III (335–330 BC) had managed to survive all the palace plots. But in 334 BC a greater problem arose. Alexander of Macedon, known as Alexander the Great, led his army against the Persian empire. Alexander's troops defeated Darius' time after time, and in 331 BC, near Babylon, Darius fled the battlefield, only to be killed by his courtiers.

Alexander took command of the entire Persian empire. He now ruled the great cities of Babylon, Susa, Persepolis, and Hamadan. The empire of Cyrus and Darius, which had survived for 150 years was at an end, and so was the great civilization of the ancient Near East.

◁ A procession of the soldiers of all nations lines the stairway at Persepolis leading into the Apadana palace. Darius I began to build the city of Persepolis. His son Xerxes continued the work and his grandson Artaxerxes completed it.

▷ The empire of Alexander the Great. When Alexander defeated Darius III at Gaugamela in 331 BC, he became lord of all the Persian territories, which extended to Central Asia and India. When he died at the age of 33, his generals divided up the vast kingdom between them. The Near East went to Seleucus, and Egypt was governed by Ptolemy.

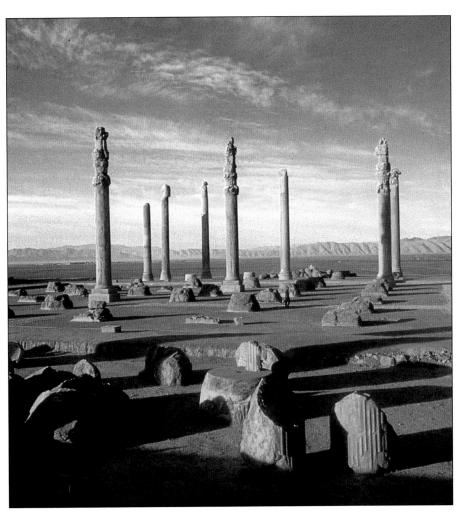

▷ The main reception hall of the Apadana palace at Persepolis. Here the king would receive important foreign visitors. The columns are almost 66ft high and have ornate capitals in the shape of bulls or lions. Columned halls were typical of Persian architecture.

◁ Alexander the Great (356–323 BC) leads his armies on a campaign. His conquests stretched from his native Macedonia and Greece to the Indus river in Asia. In battle against the Indian king Porhates, Alexander crossed the Indus. His army defeated the Indians, whose elephants panicked in battle. But Alexander's Greek troops were homesick, so he decided to begin the long march back to Greece. Reaching Babylon in 323 BC, Alexander, the invincible warrior, caught a fever and soon died.

ARCHAEOLOGY, WAR AND LOOTING

Booty was part of war in the ancient Near East. In 1159 BC the Elamites sacked Babylon, taking the sacred treasures of the Mesopotamians. The stele of Naram-Sin, Hammurabi's law code, and statues of Nana from Uruk and Marduk from Babylon were all seized. Some of these priceless treasures were never returned and were discovered, by chance, at Susa last century. Antiquities (objects from ancient times) command high prices. In 1880 three merchants were robbed in Afghanistan of their gold treasure. The thieves were found, and the Oxus treasure, named after the river where it was discovered, was given to the British Museum.

Gold objects are highly sought after, because they are easily sold. The gold treasure from the royal tombs at Kalhu was put in a bank vault in Baghdad during the 1991 Gulf War, but its fate remains unknown. Trade in stolen or illegal goods is profitable. In several countries the profits made from trading in looted antiquities have been used to finance terrorism.

▷ One of more than 1,500 objects in the Oxus treasure, which dates from the Persian empire. A gold sheet showing a man, probably a priest, wearing tight trousers and tunic. This style of clothing was worn by Persians when hunting or in battle.

▽ From the Oxus treasure. A gold roundel (sequin) that would have been sewn on to a garment. The clothing of Persian and Assyrian kings was often decorated in this way, as can be seen in the carved reliefs at Kalhu.

War damage in the Near East

The 1980–88 Iran–Iraq War and the recent Gulf War caused terrible damage to the ancient monuments of Mesopotamia. The ziggurat built by Ur-Nammu at Ur and the Northwest Palace of Ashurnasirpal at Nineveh, for example, suffered direct hits.

The destruction at many important sites that do not have great monuments will not be known for a long time. Site exploration will also be drastically limited because of the danger of unexploded landmines and bombs.

Looting of museums

Since The Gulf War, museums at Basra, Kut, Amara, and Diwaniya in the south of Iraq, and at Erbil, Dohuk, and Suleimaniya in the northern regions, have been looted and burnt. More than 4,000 objects are missing: Stone Age tools, cuneiform tablets, terracotta figurines, cylinder seals, and jewelry, covering all periods in Mesopotamian history. Descriptions of 2,000 stolen items have been recorded, but no object has so far been traced.

△ A gold model of a chariot, also from the Oxus treasure. The chariot is drawn by four horses and has on the front a head like that of the Egyptian god Bes. The model is less than 8in long.

◁ This gold bracelet from the Oxus treasure is now in the Victoria and Albert Museum, London. The hollow spaces would have been filled with colored enamels. The bracelet must have been a popular design, for a similar one is shown in the stone carvings at Persepolis as part of the Bactrian tribute. The gold jewelry from the royal tombs at Kalhu is equally beautiful.

GLOSSARY

Aceramic A term given to the Neolithic period (c.8500–7000 BC) before pottery was invented.

Akkad The northern part of Mesopotamia. The southern area was called Sumer. Akkad was named after the city Agade, but by about 1800 BC the region was called Babylonia.

Akkadian The dynasty founded by Sargon (c.2300 BC). Also the name of a Semitic language which was spoken in Mesopotamia as early as 3000 BC.

Anatolia The highland plains of present-day central Turkey.

Assyria The northern part of modern Iraq, near the border with Turkey.

Assyrian A dialect of Akkadian spoken by the Assyrians. Also the name of a dynasty which has three main periods (c.2000–612 BC).

Babylonia The region of southern Mesopotamia which was called Akkad before about 1800 BC.

Babylonian A dialect of Akkadian spoken by Babylonians. Also the name of the dynasty which ruled from about 2000 BC to 750 BC.

cuneiform The wedge-shaped script of Akkadian that was written on clay tablets and used throughout Mesopotamia and the Near East.

diorite A very hard black stone which was used to make statues.

dynasty A line of rulers usually from a single family or related through marriage.

Epi-Paleolithic The continuation of the Paleolithic or Old Stone Age culture after the last Ice Age. This period, which is sometimes called the Mesolithic, was followed by the Neolithic period.

Fertile Crescent The lands between the highland zones of Turkey and Iran and the deserts of Arabia, having 8in rainfall each year.

flint A hard stone used to make tools in the Paleolithic, Epi-Paleolithic and Neolithic periods.

figurine A small statue made from wood, ivory, clay or metal.

king list A list of the names of kings and the lengths of their reigns. The best-known is the Sumerian King List, which records the dynasties ruling the cities of Sumer until 2000 BC.

lapis lazuli A semiprecious blue stone that is only found in the mountains of Afghanistan.

law code A collection of laws recording the penalties for different crimes. The best-known law code is that of Hammurabi (c.1800 BC).

Levant The lands bordering the eastern Mediterranean, now modern Lebanon, Israel and coastal Syria.

Mesolithic The Middle Stone Age period between the Paleolithic or Old Stone Age and the Neolithic or New Stone Age. Also known as the Epi-Paleolithic.

Mesopotamia A Greek word meaning "between the rivers" and describing the lands in present-day Iraq, from south of modern Baghdad to The Gulf (Persian Gulf). The northern part of Mesopotamia was called Ákkad, the southern lands Sumer.

microliths Very small chipped stone tools that first appear in the Mesolithic period.

Natufian A culture of the Epi-Paleolithic period in the Levant (c.11,000–9300 BC) when people began to grow grain.

Neolithic The New Stone Age (c.9300–4000 BC), which was divided into the Proto-Neolithic and Aceramic periods.

obsidian A natural volcanic glass from Anatolia that is much sharper than flint and was used to make tools.

Paleolithic The Old Stone Age, which ended with the last Ice Age in about 12,000 BC. People obtained their food by hunting and gathering during this period.

pharaoh The title of the king of ancient Egypt.

Proto-Neolithic The period during the New Stone Age when grain was first grown (c.9000–8500 BC).

Semitic The language family that was widely spoken in Mesopotamia and the Near East and includes Akkadian and its dialects, Assyrian and Babylonian.

stele An upright stone or wooden slab, often decorated with carvings or bearing inscriptions.

Sumer The southern lands of Mesopotamia, reaching to The Gulf (Persian Gulf), that were occupied by the Sumerians. The plain north of modern Baghdad was called Akkad.

Sumerian The language which was spoken in Sumer by the Sumerians in about 4000 BC. Sumerian does not belong to the Semitic language family.

tablet A small flat slab, usually made of clay, on which an inscription in cuneiform would be written.

tell An Arabic word for a mound made by the remains of ancient settlements. Often part of a place-name, as in Tell Madhhur.

ziggurat A high tower built of stepped platforms with a temple at the top.

FURTHER READING

General works and picture books

William W. Hallo, *The Ancient Near East: A History* (Harcourt Brace), 1971.
Amiet Pierce, *Art of the Ancient Near East* (Abrams), 1980.
Georges Roux, *Ancient Iraq* (Viking Penguin), 1993.
Jonathan Tubb, *Bible Lands* (Knopf), 1991.

Adult reference books

John Baines, *Atlas of Ancient Egypt* (Facts On File) 1980.
O. R. Gurney, *The Hittites* (Viking Penguin) 1991.
Joan C. Oates, *Babylon* (Thames & Hudson) 1986.
Michael Roaf, *Cultural Atlas of Mesopotamia and the Ancient Near East* (Facts on File) 1990.
John Rogerson, *The Atlas of the Bible* (Facts On File) 1984.

GAZETTEER

The gazetteer lists places and features, such as rivers or mountains, found on the maps. Each has a separate entry including a page and grid reference number. For example:

Abu Gosh 20 B2

Where a place also has an alternative name form this name is added to the entry before the page number. For example:

Alexandria (Ghazni) 89 E2

All features are shown in italic type. For example:

Anshan, d. 52 C2

A letter after the feature describes the kind of feature:

d. district; *f.* feature; *i.* island; *mt.* mountain; *mts.* mountains; *r.* river

Abu Gosh 20 B2
Abu Hureyra 20 C3
Abu Salabikh 32 A3, 41 C2
Abu Salem 20 B2
Abydos 89 A3
Adab 41 C2, 47, 54 B2, 56 C2, 60 B2
Agade 52 B3, 56 C2
Aijalon 66 B2
Ain Ghazal 20 B2
Ain Mallaha 20 B2
Ain Gev I 20 B2
Akkad, d. 41 C2, 52 C3
Akshak 41 C2
al-Azizyeh 60 A3
al-Khiam 20 B2
Al-Untash-Napirisha (Choga Zanbil) 47
Alalah 58 B2
Aleppo 58 B2, 65 B2, 72 B3
Alexandria 89 B2
Alexandria 89 C2
Alexandria 89 D1
Alexandria 89 E2
Alexandria 89 F1
Alexandria (Ghazni) 89 E2

Alexandria (Herat) 89 E2
Alexandria (Kandahar) 89 E2
Alexandria Eschata (Kokand) 89 F3
Alexandropolis 89 D2
Ali Kosh 20 E2, 29 E1
Alps, mts. 14 H6
Amanus Mts 41 A3
Amid 72 C3
Ammon, d. 66 C3, 72 B2
Amu Darya, r. 11 G3, 14 F3
An Nafud, f. 11 C1
Ana 65 C2, 72 C2
Anatolia d. 10 B3, 14 B3, 20 A3, 25 B3
Ankara 89 B3
Anshan, d. 52 C2
Aornus 89 E2
Apamea 29 B2
Aphek 66 A3
Apku 47, 65 C2
Arabia, d. 11 D1, 14 C1, 84 B1
Arachosia, d. 85 F2, 89 E1
Arad of Beth-yeroham 66 B2
Aram, d. 66 C4, 72 B2
Araxes, r. 89 C3
Arbil 47, 58 D2, 65 C2, 72 D3, 89 C2
Aria, d. 85 F2, 89 E2
Armanum 52 A3
Armenia, d. 84 C3, 89 C2
Arpachiyeh 29 D2
Arrapha 65 C2, 72 D2
Arslantepe 29 C3
Asharne 72 B2
Ashdod 66 A2, 72 B1
Ashikli Huyuk 20 A4
Ashkelon 29 B1
Ashur 41 C3, 47, 52 B3, 56 B3, 58 D2, 65 C2, 72 D2
Asia Minor, d. 89 B2
Assyria, d. 72 C3, 84 C2
Awan 41 D2

Babylon 47, 52 B3, 54 A3, 56 C2, 58 D1, 60 A3, 65 C1, 72 D2, 82 C3, 84 C2, 89 C2
Babylonia, d. 72 D2, 84 C2, 89 C2
Bactria, d. 85 F2, 89 E2
Bad-tibira 41 C2, 54 C2
Badakhshan, d. 85 G2
Baghouz 29 C2
Baladruz 60 B4
Balikh, r. 52 B3
Basta 20 B2

Beer-sheba 66 A2
Beidha 20 B2
Beisamoun 20 B2
Belbasi 20 A3
Beth-Horon 66 B2
Beth-Shan 66 B3
Beth-Shemesh 66 A2
Bethel 66 B2
Bisutun 84 D2
Black Sea 11 C3, 14 B3, 15 F6, 25 B3, 82 B4, 84 B3, 89 B3
Borim 66 B3
Borsippa 47, 54 A3, 56 C2, 60 A3, 72 D2
Bouqras 20 C3
Byblos 29 B2, 41 A3, 58 B2, 72 B2

Cafer Huyuk 20 C4
Can Hasan 20 A3
Cappadocia, d. 84 B3
Carchemish 58 B2, 65 B2, 72 B3
Caria, d. 84 A2
Carmania, d. 84 E1, 89 D1
Carmel, Mt 20 B2, 66 B3
Caspian Sea 11 E3, 14 D3, 15 G6, 20 E4, 25 D3, 29 E3, 41 E3, 52 C4, 72 E3, 82 D4, 84 D3, 89 D2
Caucasus Mts 11 D3, 82 C4
Cedar Mt 52 A3
Chagar Bazar 29 C2
Chatal Huyuk 29 A2
Chayonu 20 C4
Choga Bonut 20 E2
Choga Mami 29 D1
Choga Zanbil see Al-Untash-Napirisha
Chorasmia, d. 85 E2
Cilicia, d. 82 B3, 89 B2
Crete, i. 84 A2, 89 A2
Cyprus, i. 10 B2, 20 A3, 25 A2, 29 A2, 52 A3, 72 A2, 84 B2, 89 B2
Cyrene 89 A2

Damascus 66 C4, 72 B2, 89 B2
Dasht-e Kavir, f. 11 E2
Dasht-e Lut, f. 11 F2
Dead Sea 15 F6, 29 B1, 41 A2, 52 A1, 58 B1, 66 B2, 72 B1, 84 B2
Deh-i No 47
Der 41 C2, 60 B3, 72 D2
Derbent 89 E2
Dilbat 54 A3, 56 C2
Dilmun, d. 52 C2
Diyala, r. 41 C3, 58 D2, 65 C2

Dor 66 A3
Dothan 66 B3
Drangiana, d. 84 E1
Dur-Katlimmu 65 B2
Dur-Kurigalzu 47, 60 A3, 65 C1, 72 D2
Dur-Sharrukin (Khorsabad) 47, 72 D3

Ebla 41 A3, 52 A3, 58 B2
Edom, d. 66 B1, 72 B1
Egypt, d. 10 B1, 14 B1, 52 A2, 72 A1, 82 B2, 84 A1, 89 A1
Elam, d. 11 E2, 41 D2, 52 C2, 72 E2, 84 D2
Elburz Mts 11 E2
Emesa 89 B2
Emutbal, d. 56 C2
Eridu 29 E1, 41 D2, 47, 54 C1, 56 C1
Eshnunna 41 C2, 56 C2
Euphrates, r. 11 C2, 14 C2, 20 D2, 29 C2, 32 B1, 41 B3, 47, 52 B3, 54 A2, 56 B2, 58 C2, 60 A2, 65 B2, 72 C2, 82 C3, 84 C2, 89 C2

Galilee, Sea of 66 B3
Gandara, d. 85 F2
Ganj Dareh 20 E3
Gaugamela 89 C2
Gaza 66 A2, 72 B1, 89 B2
Gedrosia, d. 89 E1
Gezer 66 A2
Ghazni see Alexandria
Gibeon 66 B2
Gilgal 66 B3
Girsu 41 D2, 54 C2, 56 C2, 60 B2
Gobi, f. 14 J6
Godin Tepe 41 D3
Granicus 89 A3
Great Zab, r. 11 D2, 20 D3, 41 C3, 58 D2
Great Arad 66 B2
Greece, d. 89 A2
Gritille 20 C3
Gulf, The 11 E1, 14 D1, 15 B2, 20 E1, 25 D1, 41 D1, 47, 52 C2, 56 D1, 60 C1, 72 E1, 82 D2, 84 D1, 89 D1
Gutium, d. 41 C3

Habur, r. 11 C2, 20 C3, 29 C2, 41 B3, 52 B3, 58 C2
Hacilar 20 A3
Hajji Muhammad 29 D1
Hama 29 B2, 72 B2
Hamadan 82 D3, 84 D2, 89 C2

Hamazi 41 C3
Hamman 47
Hana, d. 56 B3
Haradum 56 B3
Harhar 72 E2
Harlicarnassus 89 A2
Harran 58 C2, 65 B2, 72 C3, 82 C3
Hasanlu 29 D2, 41 C3
Hatula 20 B2
Hazor 66 B4
Hecatompylos 89 D2
Hejaz, f. 11 C1
Herat see Alexandria
Himalayas, mts. 14 J5
Hindanu 72 C2
Hit 65 C1
Huleh, Lake 66 B4

Imleihiyeh 60 B4
Indus, d. 85 F1
Indus, r. 14 F1, 82 F2, 85 F1, 89 E1
Ionia, d. 84 A2
Isin 54 B2, 56 C2, 60 B2
Israel, d. 66 B3, 72 B2
Issus 89 B2

Jarmo 20 D3, 29 D2
Jericho 20 B2, 66 B2
Jerusalem 66 B2, 72 B1, 82 B3, 84 B2, 89 B2
Jezreel 66 B3
Joppa 66 A3
Jordan, r. 66 B3
Judah, d. 66 B2, 72 B1

Kalhu 47, 65 C2, 72 D3
Kandahar see Alexandria
Kar-Tukulti-Ninurta 47, 65 C2
Kara Kum, f. 11 F3
Karim Shahir 20 D3
Kebara 20 B2
Khafajeh 52 B3
Khan Bani Sa'ad 60 A3
Khorsabad see Dur-Sharrukin
Kilizu 65 C2
Kiriath-jearim 66 B2
Kish 41 C2, 47, 52 B3, 54 A3, 56 C2, 60 A3
Kisurra 54 B2
Kizil Irmak, r. 11 B3, 14 B3, 52 A4, 58 B3
Kokand see Alexandria Eschata
Kokola 89 E1
Kul Tepe 29 D2
Kulishkhinash 65 B2
Kutha 54 A3, 56 C2, 60 A3, 72 D2

INDEX